SAILING HOME

SAILING HOME

Honduras towards England in a Small Boat

PETER HANCOCK

Drawings by David Wright

THOMAS REED PUBLICATIONS
A DIVISION OF THE ABR COMPANY LIMITED

First published in the UK 2001
by Thomas Reed Publications,
a Division of The ABR Company Limited

British Library Cataloguing in Publication Data
A catalogue record for this book
is available from the British Library

ISBN 0 901281 99 9

Produced by Omega Profiles Ltd, SP11 7RW
Printed and bound in Great Britain by MPG Books Ltd, Bodmin, Cornwall

Thomas Reed Publications
A DIVISION OF THE ABR COMPANY
The Barn, Ford Farm, Bradford Leigh, Bradford-on-Avon
Wiltshire BA15 2RP, United Kingdom
E-mail: sales@abreed.demon.co.uk

REED'S is the trade mark of The ABR Company Ltd.

Peter Hancock has also written:

Sailing Out of Silence: 30,000 miles in a Small Boat
(Waterline Books, 1995)

*Sailing Into Sunshine: 5,000 miles
through the Caribbean and Gulf of Mexico*
(Waterline Books, 1997)

and is Associate Editor of Nigel Calder's

The Cruising Guide to the Northwest Caribbean
(International Marine Publishing, 1991)

NOTE

Some material in this book first appeared
in the magazine *Yachting Monthly*.

To Charles Danforth,
who has sailed down a dark river
and found a sunlit sea.

Down to Gehenna or up to the Throne,
He travels the fastest who travels alone.

KIPLING *The Winners*

Neither sleepy nor deaf men are fit to
travel quite alone.

FRANCIS GALTON *The Art of Travel*

Acknowledgements

I wish to thank Nigel and Terrie Calder, whose cool heads and capable hands helped me to cross troubled waters; and Sarah Miller, Joseph Miller and Esther Hancock for making sure that after seven years away from England in a small boat I still had a home to sail back to.

Contents

1	Philips' Atlas	13
2	The Going Back	18
3	Mario's and Izabal	23
4	Three Reefs and One Extra	29
5	Selling a Shotgun	37
6	Up, Down and English	45
7	Coxen's Hole to The Settlement	53
8	Tommy Atkins in Sepia	62
9	Trujillo Bay	66
10	Cochino Grande	70
11	Chachahuate	77
12	Dolours and Scents	82
13	Good Friday in Guatemala	91
14	The Venus Delivery	95
15	Dawn Rescue	106
16	Fingers and Thumbs	113
17	Barracuda and Baron Bliss	117
18	*You and I*	125
19	Cay Caulker	128
20	Hold-up on Albert Street	134
21	Meeting a Survivor	137
22	Simon Goes to Paradise	142
23	A Promise in French Harbour	147
24	Fall of a Swallow	151
25	To Florida	158
26	José	161
27	Strong Wind off Bermuda	172
28	Coldfinger	176
29	Christie	182
30	Down for the Third Time	186
31	Shark in Aspic	191
32	Sailing Home	199
33	Epilogue	206

Appendices

1	*Kylie*	207
2	Glossary of Nautical Terms	211

Charts

1	Guatemala: Bahia de Amatique to Lago Izabal	24
2	Caribbean Sea: Rio Dulce to the Bay Isands of Honduras	43
3	Gulf of Honduras: South-west Utila and adjacent cays	48
4	Roatan and Los Cayos Cochinos	54
5	Los Cayos Cochinos	73
6	Caribbean Sea: Tucacas, Venezuela, to Livingston, Guatemala	97
7	Caribbean Sea and N Atlantic Ocean: Bay Islands to Bermuda	173
8	North Atlantic Ocean: Mean Maximum Ice Limit	179
9	Ireland: Bull Rock to Baltimore	204

Charts courtesy of Nigel Calder

1

Philips' Atlas

With a raw north-east wind whirling snow into his eyes, in April 1936 a small but greatly daring seaman named Dod Orsborne put out from Dover in the trawler *Girl Pat*. The ship's owners thought Skipper Orsborne was setting off to fish Home Waters. Not until months later did they discover he had stolen away with their trawler to cruise the Atlantic for his own pleasure.

After weeks in which she was not certainly sighted nor heard of, *Girl Pat* was posted missing. Then, one morning in autumn the *Daily Express* came out with the news that the trawler and its starving crew had been towed into Georgetown in British Guiana under armed escort. So ended a transatlantic voyage of six thousand miles.

Orsborne was sent back to England as a Distressed British Seaman and sentenced to twelve years' hard labour. To a small boy in short trousers, though, he seemed a hero.

I first read about Orsborne's voyage when at the age of nine I was sent to fetch my gran's asthma cure from a drawer which two years previously had been lined with the *Express*. What caught and held my interest in the story was that Orsborne had found his way around the Atlantic using only a schoolboy's atlas. This revelation sent me into frequent daydreams, which were broken now and then by bouts of the fidgets.

In the course of one of these daydreams I was steering *Girl Pat* through a stiff gale off Cape Finisterre when a mountainous green wave burst into the wheelhouse, causing me to spill porridge onto a flannelette sheet which my mother was winding through the mangle.

"Stop those antics, for Heaven's sake!" she cried.

By clamping my hands between my knees I kept my limbs quiet for a while, but, as if in protest at these restrictions, later in the same day my chest and back broke out in tremendous heat lumps.

"What the dickens has the lad been getting up to?" wheezed Gran suspiciously from her pillow as Mum dabbed the red blotches with calamine lotion. The charge of bad behaviour was no surprise, for Cleanliness was said to be next to Godliness in those days, so that coming out in pimples was as likely to be put down to a collapse of morality as a disorder of the blood. "The next thing you know," Gran went on darkly, "all his tubes will be blocked up; he'd better sniff salt water up his nose before he goes from bad to worse."

Though this form of purging was common, it did not find favour in all quarters of the family.

"Pah! That'll do him more harm than ever," cried an aunt up in Liverpool on being told of Gran's remedy. "Salt water is the very cause of his upset."

This aunt was a bony widow in a beaded black dress who spoke always from a rocking-chair in the shadows. Her husband had been lost in a storm off Cape Hatteras, after which tragedy she hardly ever kissed anyone. According to what she went on to say to Mum, my blood had been infected by tales of the sea told by men who left their wives without a ha'penny to buy even porridge oats, let alone sugar to go on it. To me she did not speak quite so sternly, but I feared her almost as much as I feared Captain Hook who lurked in my wardrobe.

In June 1945, months before my sixteenth birthday but only weeks before my schooldays ended, my parents told me that it was about time I left off drawing *Girl Pats* and instead wrote letters of application to – to take their usual example – banks. Not wanting to go against them, I gave in. We sold off most of my school books to help towards the cost of a clerical grey suit from the Fifty-shilling (£2.50 or $4.00*) Tailors, but I made up my mind to hold on to the school atlas, and I did. At nights, instead of reading about the difference between stocks and shares like any other junior bank clerk with a shred of ambition should have been doing, I would hang up the clerical suit in my wardrobe – from which Captain Hook had not long departed – turn to page 13 of the Thirty-third, 1940 edition of George Philips' New Modern School Atlas, and carry on with my navigations of the Atlantic Ocean as pictured by Mollweide's Homolographic Projection and reduced by Philips to a scale of one inch to sixty million. Parting with the atlas, it seemed to me then, would have cut down my chances of actually navigating the Atlantic to nought.

My days in the bank were spent on a high stool opposite Rhoda, a slow-speaking blonde of my own age. She wore shimmering white

---

* £1 = $1.60 throughout this book.

". . . a bony widow in a beaded black dress."

blouses and had a liking for cream doughnuts. To me, Rhoda was a
puzzle but was also a challenge. The frosty looks which came across
the desk from her faraway blue eyes seemed nothing but a try-on, not
part of her doughnut-eating self at all. I laughed-off the frosty glances
and tried to uncover the warm heart which lay beneath. Though the cut
of my fifty-shilling suit was not nearly sharp enough to break through

15

her defences, my cheque-spikings sometimes cracked them. At the start of the working day the spikes were always standing halfway between us like a steel fence, but by the time she sank her teeth into the first doughnut at ten-thirty I would have jiggled them as near to the shimmering blouse as I could possibly get without falling from my stool. Though Rhoda could not have failed to notice these advances, she hardly ever shoved the spikes back.

Having dipped my nib into an inkwell and posted a cheque in the ledger, I would launch myself towards her on the pretext of spiking it, gazing earnestly into her eyes as I zoomed in.

To the frowns of the senior clerks who saw it happen, the cheque itself would then wander from its course, sometimes becoming holed so far off-centre as to puncture the figures which came after the £ sign, but Rhoda herself didn't seem to be at all put out by these mutilations. I think she secretly relished them.

It all ended on a morning when she bought me a runny jam doughnut to go with her cream one. Made suddenly misty-eyed by this kindness, I launched myself towards her shimmering blouse so intently that the cheque overshot the spike and the spike went into my wrist, where it stuck fast. Rhoda was so impressed by this happening that she dropped her doughnut into the inkwell and passed out.

Still sketching *Girl Pats*, I left the bank in some haste and made my way to the offices of a shipping company in London, where, by informing a doctor in lopsided spectacles that my hearing was normal although all the known world outside my family circle had been shrieking for years it was anything but, I bluffed my way through a medical. Before the year was over my father had bound me to the company as an apprentice and I had crossed the Atlantic six times in a vessel furnished with hundreds of charts which covered not only the North and South Atlantic but three other oceans as well. The charts were stupendously larger than any to be found in the *New Modern School Atlas*, the largest being five feet wide.

Although in later years it was glanced into from time to time so as to answer questions such as whether our house in Lowestoft lay north or south of the part of Birmingham where my heat lumps had blossomed, I did not study the atlas closely again until the fifteenth year of my marriage. By then my career as a merchant sailor had come to an end long since, but I still liked the sea, as too did my wife, whose name was Pip. Sitting side by side in front of the fire after our children had been put to bed and read to, we turned the pages of the atlas and traced out the voyages we would make together in the boat we planned to get, but before these tracings could be lifted off George Philips' by now quite grimy and unmodern atlas and copied onto proper sea-charts, Pip sickened and died. As happens even today in the pages of the novel, the dreams lived on and became stronger, and so a year after her death I bought a small but sturdy sailing-boat named *Kylie* with the idea of doing the travels which Pip and I had planned to make together, sharing whatever might come. Though death had parted us, I believed that by making these voyages attentively and alone I could share my travels with her in a spiritual way. I wanted the voyages to be as fulfilling as – for much of its course – our marriage had been.

Time alters all, but over the years this ambition has changed less than most.

In September 1985 I set off from England by myself and, after cruising the Mediterranean and Black Seas, in January 1989 crossed the Atlantic to the West Indies, entering an area which in the eighteenth century was called the New World and sometimes still is. So far, the travels in *Kylie* had given me a number of interesting experiences, most of which had been agreeable, but the spiritual traffic between Pip and me had been disappointingly thin and bitty. The fault, I knew, was mine. Among other pleasant diversions, I'd been having too much wild wassail and thick-cut tobacco.

By the summer of 1989 *Kylie* had cruised those parts of the New World which curve north and west from the island of Antigua to the Outer Banks of Carolina. In September of the year I sailed south and west to the Mississippi delta, and on Christmas Day made a landfall on the Yucatán peninsula of Mexico. At the earnest request of an insurer whose Jaguar was forever plunging into water-filled East Anglian ditches, two of these American passages had been made with a companion, but for most of the time I was still sailing by myself, listening for Pip.

2

The Going Back

Living alone in a cabin the size of a double bed, with all the headroom – and some of the odours – of an understairs boot-cupboard, can be a pleasant experience, and for most of the time it is, but when people suggest that I must surely meet a few of life's little hardships while sailing *Kylie*, I admit to having had one or two problems with my water and, to a curiously inter-related extent, with my beer.

The beer cans are stowed below the waterline in a deep and narrow bilge, at a temperature which, in the areas of ocean lying outside the tropical and sub-tropical zones, can range from below freezing point to 20°C (68°F). To anyone like me, happy to drink at local room-temperatures bitter beer on draught in England and canned lager anywhere else, this temperature-range will not seem too wide. When *Kylie* sailed into the Caribbean, though, the bilge temperature rose to 30°C (86°F), which so greatly overheated the beer cans that now and then they blew up.

The most upsetting explosions happened while *Kylie* was at anchor off a small town in Yucatán. I had sailed into the anchorage at the end of a trying overnight passage, during which I had been bucking currents that had foxed not only me in my small boat but also – if the quantity of wrecks shown on the chart was anything to go by – masters of much larger vessels, many of which had been carried so far adrift from their courses that they had run aground. On the chart the wrecks looked like the skeletons of whales which had impaled themselves on the reefs in an act of mass suicide. The suicidal urge was familiar, for several times that night I had felt like doing the same.

As a result of these close encounters with reefs and a painful brush with the engine's starting-handle, I had bruised an elbow and burnt three fingers. When *Kylie* was firmly anchored and the deck had been tidied I went down into the cabin to seek some balm and refreshment, but in the course of digging them out of the bilge two cans of Budweiser blew up in my face. At once the likelihood of discovering refreshment on board *Kylie* evaporated among lager suds and low curses, so I rowed my dinghy to the town jetty to look for them on the beach. Here, along a sandy path which ran at right angles to the jetty was a thatched *palapa* in which a hammock was swinging in the trade wind, conch shells were gleaming pinkly from the walls and bottled beer was being handed out from an ice box.

I sank into the hammock and drank some.

"What doing here?" seemed to say a bird with green wings and a blue tongue while peeling a cashew. "Am sailing south towards Belize," I told it from the corner of my mouth, "along with the Calder family in their *Nada*, investigating reefs and islands." On learning this, the bird slowly closed an eye and yawned.

Shortly afterwards I gave much the same information to a doctor of medicine who had flown down from Idaho for a two-week Central American holiday and who now, six months later, was still in Mexico, happily putting off any idea of going back. Apart from a light sprinkle of puce dots, his shirt was the same bright blue as the bird's tongue but his eyes took in more of what I was telling him than the bird's had been when I had been giving it the same message. His reactions, too, were quicker. He suddenly grasped my left hand in his own left hand and pressed down hard on a ganglion at the base of my thumb, an act which caused me to wince.

"Eureka!" he cried, in the uplifting tone used by Archimedes in his bath. "You are incubating a serious problem down below . . .!"

Down below what? I was lying in a hammock only inches from the ground and he was looking down at me from a stool, so it was difficult to know if the malady he had in mind was hatching out in the whole of my body or just the parts of it which lay below my belt. Whichever he had meant, I brushed off his words as a ridiculous diversion, for our beer bottles were now empty and, by my reckoning, the next round was his.

Weeks after this encounter I sailed *Kylie* southward from Belize to Guatemala and anchored in the Rio Dulce, where the so-called "serious problem" found itself a local habitation and a name. During a night of heavy rain I went on deck to ease my bladder. Under the awning at the guardrail I made a slight re-alignment to my penis and waited for my water to mingle with the rain. After a while I frowned. A commendable stream was coursing from the end of my dick but not a drop of it was being pumped out by me. I thought liberating thoughts, but no water came out. My pump was powerless and, try as I might, I could not bring it into action. In all senses of the expression, the issue was out of my hands.

During the whole of the next day hardly any of my water saw the light of the sun or – when retention went on after dark – a number of forty-watt bulbs. The taking of some pink and white tablets unblocked my urethra before the next sunrise but did not dissolve the fears of prostate cancer, which by then were clogging up my brain. To put an end to these uncertainties I boarded an early flight to England, where I hoped a doctor with a quieter taste in shirts might tell me how many weeks would go by before I had to go to my grave.

"Hang on! I thought you were cruising the West Indies!" a tall friend with shrewd eyes remarked in the bar of the Lord Nelson at Southwold, where rain had followed me and was coming down as heavily as ever. "What brings you back to England in this rotten weather?"

"I need some spare parts," I said, "for the boat."

Outside the pub, breakers were straddling the groynes and spending themselves on the shingle. Swollen by rain and a northerly gale, the River Blyth was surging into the North Sea at six knots. St Edmund's church clock stood at ten to three and my mouth was feeling dry.

In the doctor's surgery hung a painting of foaming waters entitled *Rise Time*. As no-one in the waiting-room had looked a day under sixty, the picture seemed well chosen. Drawing hope from it, I turned up my deaf-aid and prepared to learn my fate.

"Three days ago I couldn't pass water," I said to the doctor, "but in Guatemala they gave me some tablets called Desflam and Bactrin, and quite soon after taking them I managed a small piddle. What d'you make of it?"

"What is the pressure like now?"

"Back to normal, I'd say."

The doctor leaned forward in his chair and said, "You're sure?"

"Well, it comes out without too much urging from me."

"That's all right for now, then:" he said, leaning back, "so why have you come to see me?"

"Can't say . . . Don't know . . . May I have some sleeping-pills, though, now that I'm here? Enough for, say, six months?"

He kept his eyes on my face and smiled.

"When I lie down," I explained, "my mind starts revving up."

He began tapping out a prescription on his computer.

"Why did you get that painting?" I asked.

"To induce tranquillity."

"You know, I knew you'd say that," I said. "As soon as I saw it I said to myself 'He's hung that picture up there so as to calm his patients' minds'."

"The devil I did," said the doctor; "I put it there to calm mine."

Outside Gatwick Departures my son-in-law Joe loaded my bags onto a trolley and Sarah gave me a kiss. Over her shoulder I saw that my TO GUATEMALA via HOUSTON labels were fluttering.

"Please don't hang about; get back home and walk the dogs."

Joe trundled the trolley towards the entrace lobby.

"I can hear something rattling," Sarah said into my better ear.

"It might be the sleeping-tablets; I used the cotton wool from the bottle to polish my glasses."

I stood apart, and said "I really will be all right. I'll just dawdle around Guatemala and Honduras, help Nigel to finish off his cruising guide, and then I'll sail *Kylie* home."

"With a crew this time, Dad? "

"I'll be sailing into Southwold next summer, dear."

She made out that my answer was good enough, and she waved as they drove off.

The next lie was spoken at the customs desk. I was taking a bagful of boat equipment to Guatemala and was hoping to claim back the tax on it on the grounds that for most of the previous five years I had been living aboard *Kylie* in the Mediterranean, the USA and the West Indies, and was therefore an expatriate.

I slid the tax-refund forms across the counter, towards a man whose glistening bald head was underlined by heavy black-framed spectacles which exactly paralleled his thick black eyebrows.

"Now, sir," he said, fingers drumming on the counter, "are you a resident of the United Kingdom?"

"No, I have a house but it's rented out; I live aboard my boat."

"You own a property, therefore you are a resident," he cried, bringing his fist down like a gavel.

"That's as unreasonable as saying that everyone who owns a garage has therefore got a car."

"It's a terrible hard world, sir," he said, sweeping the forms into a waste bin, "but that's how it is."

Bearing in mind what comes out of volcanoes, this assessment of the nature of the world is open to doubt, but I have noticed that it is often on the lips of people whose job in life is to make it more difficult for others. So far, the hardships that officials have threatened to inflict – and in some cases have actually inflicted – upon me and my boat have included: being woken at two in the morning to check documents (Turkey); lacerating the hull (Greece, Turkey and Sardinia); being shot at (Honduras); incarceration (USA); starvation (Bulgaria); mislaying mail (Virgin Islands) or pretending to do so (Guatemala); forbidding landing (Spain); and making muddles. This last has happened in every country I have been to except the Irish Republic, where the *gardai* mingle their instructions with helpful comments on the quality of the local fish and convey them solely – and, as often as not, poetically – by word of mouth.

Not a lot of Guatemalan officials look like brainboxes because so few of them can afford glasses but I already knew that many were rather good at making muddles. An alluring immigration officer in a silky white blouse like Rhoda's had caused me to scurry back and forth between the Department of Finance and the airport to have re-typed a document which she had alleged was gravely defective but which turned out in the end to lack only a couple of commas. If re-entering Guatemala was going to be as upsetting as leaving it had been, I could see my nervous system going wonky in addition to my urinary. At least at Gatwick one could feel pretty sure that if another hopeful expat with boat-bits handed the same set of forms to a different brainbox in the next booth on the following day he would meet with the same equally depressing response, though not perhaps such a terse one.

At three in the morning at Guatemala city airport I lumped my bags off a conveyor belt and sweated. In the warm, rancid air two silent men in peaked caps with the Spanish for "Anything to declare?" hanging invisibly about them were eyeing the passengers who were straggling through the barriers ahead. An American travel-club with archaeological leanings wound towards the exit. I fell into step with a man and woman from Chicago and made out with them under the eyes of the officials, all the while talking with more liveliness than knowledge about the Mayan ruins in which the interior of Guatemala abounded and towards which the travel club was directing its footsteps.

My own path, they discovered when our bags had passed unmolested through the barriers only to be torn from our hands by a horde of panting porters lying in wait on the other side, lay in a different direction. They were going up-country to the ruins, but I was going to the Rio Dulce and down it, by and by, to the sea.

3
Mario's and Izabal

Guatemala has two hundred miles of coastline, most of it on the Pacific Ocean. Its Caribbean coast is so very short that if you place one point of a pair of dividers on the mouth of the river which marks the frontier with Belize on the chart and put the other on the Honduran border, you will span only forty miles. This seaboard is made up of little else than the Bahia de Amatique, a tiny back-pocket of the Caribbean Sea. If it weren't for the attractions of another river which flows into the south-western part of the bay, most cruising boats would pass Guatemala without stopping.

This second river, the Rio Dulce, idles through jungly lowlands before running across a shallow bar into the sea, but on the way it makes some forceful contrasts, issuing into the Bahia de Amatique with a dramatic flourish, twisting through a deep gorge. By motor-sailing up this gorge, boats can reach El Golfete, where the river broadens into a lake, and beyond it Lago Izabal, a miniature sea twenty-five miles long and ten wide. The two lakes are fed by a number of dark and winding rivers, some of them navigable.

A quivering bus set me down at the only bridge across the river, between the villages of Fronteras and Relleno, and soon a launch was skimming across two miles of tawny water to where lay *Kylie* at Mario's marina.

I unlaced the boat covers, took off my shoes and went below. Though hot and still, the air in the cabin was not heavy. I ran my fingers over the red leatherette berth-cushions, the chart table, and the slatted chart rack below the deckhead. They came away clean. Lowering my head, I squeezed past the tubular steel mast-support, knelt on the knee-high bin in the forecabin – which I sometimes called the forepeak – and poked my head out of the forehatch.

Bearing a wilted plant, Daphne padded by.

"Gracious! You're back!"

"Yes, this minute!"

Why was it such a pleasure to see her? She wore her hair in a chignon

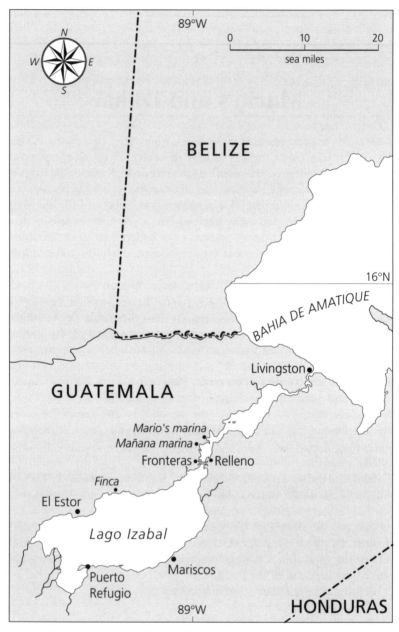

Chart 1: Guatemala: Bahia de Amatique to Lago Izabal.

and was classically beautiful, and was, in everyone's opinion, a brick.

"Thanks for keeping the cabin so clean of mould," I said.

"No problem!" said Daphne. "Chay opened the hatches every day and pumped the bilge. But how are *you*? How did things go?

"Better than expected. But, Daphne, thick-cut marmalade has gone up to 65p (97 $^1/_2$ c) a jar, and so, you know, I just had to come back to a less jammy way of life."

Mario's was run by Barrie and Daphne Hartley, who in a few months had transformed a neglected and rather gloomy peninsula into a sunnier but still shady place, with a wooden walkway along the waterside which gave moorings for a dozen boats. Most of the boats were from the United States but others came from more distant countries: Canada, Sweden, Holland, Germany and – astonishingly to me – Switzerland, a country which, till then, I had not thought of as having ports.

Nada, the Spanish for "Nothing", home port New Orleans and owned by Nigel and Terrie Calder, lay next to *Kylie*. She was a white-hulled, double-ended ketch with a short bowsprit. I knew her well.

Before sunset I eased *Kylie* from her berth, anchored off in the river, rigged the windscoop and waited for *Nada*'s crew to come back from their journey to the interior. Parrots flew in pairs from bank to bank, lights came on in the marina, and on a nearby spur of land a Mayan family began eating rice and beans. By degrees the sky turned indigo. I pinched the wick of the brass cabin-lamp, held a lighted match to it and wondered how the Calders were getting on.

With *Kylie* and me as smaller, older and – from time to time – rather faltering companions, for months Nigel and Terrie had been surveying the north-western Caribbean in *Nada*, gathering data for Nigel's cruising guide. Our boats had foraged most of the harbours and anchorages which lie between the Yucatán peninsula of Mexico and the Rio Dulce, but while I had been away in England they and their two infant children had been sight-seeing Mayan ruins. If Nigel meant to keep to his schedule, it was high time for us to move on from the mainland to the Bay Islands of Honduras.

Tired but not tetchy after six hours in a bus, the Calders came back to their boat in the afternoon of the following day. Soon they had motored *Nada* out of the marina and were anchored astern of *Kylie*, with their awning rippling in the breeze and three quarters of the crew jumping overboard for swims.

"Peter!" cried Terrie as I breast-stroked sedately towards them.

"Just look at *me*!" spluttered Pippin, dog-paddling. "I'm swimming without my ring!"

"You're a monster!" shouted three-year-old Paul before puffing out his cheeks till they bulged as roundly as his pneumatic armlets.

I climbed aboard *Nada* just in time to help Nigel drink a potful of Earl Grey.

"Hum!" he began, blinking amiably through his spectacles. "Before leaving for the Bay Islands we'll need to spend a day or two investigating Lago Izabal."

We ghosted past the now deserted spur where the Mayans had been eating their meal, and soon our boats were gliding under the high concrete bridge, past women washing clothes in the old way by walloping them on stones. A mile past their washplace I anchored off Castillo de San Felipe in three fathoms, just outside what I imagined to be musket range of the battlements, but when I looked at it more closely the castle seemed far too dainty to be formidable. Red pantiled roofs lined a trim courtyard and though the outer walls rose high above *Nada*'s masthead they did not look at all repulsive. Yet centuries ago they must have deterred others, for our boats were lying where the captains of Spanish treasure fleets would have felt safe from attacks by Sir Henry Morgan and other brethren of the coast. While Mayan slaves loaded the galleons with gold and silver taken from the mines in the mountains which loomed in the south, their masters would have rested easy under those pantiles, protected by the cannon of the Castillo de San Felipe. Nigel said that, for all its dainty quaintness, the castle would have been a truly tough nut to crack, and that attacking the galleons would have been none too easy, either. The cannon were pointing downriver, ready to fire grapeshot at any buccaneers who managed to steal up through the gorge in boats which, in most cases, would have been even smaller than my 26-foot *Kylie*. Warned of the coming attack by lookouts, the galleons would have then been warped a couple of hundred yards past the castle and onto Lago Izabal. If any buccaneers who had not by then been peppered by grapeshot tried to get at the galleons they would have run into a huge chain which the defenders would have winched up from the riverbed between the castle and the opposite shore.

Doing five knots under engine against a current, *Nada* forged smartly through the narrows where the chain had once lain, on to Lago Izabal. Wearing only a genoa, *Kylie* followed her more slowly, the eager waves jaunting ahead. Twenty-five miles of Lago Izabal opened before us as our bows lifted to an oily swell. Encouraged by the brisk wind in the narrows and the sight of distant mountains, I wanted to set more sail but was put off by the sight of miles of fishing nets buoyed by blue plastic bottles that were difficult to spot in the dark green water made darker by an overcast sky.

The lake broadened, the hill forests abeam became distant whalebacks and the nets fewer. At last I was able to goosewing a second genoa and hope for a speedy passage to Puerto Refugio, a long-jawed inlet at the south-western end of the lake, but before mid-day the wind fell light and soon *Kylie* was making barely two knots under the ghoster and *Nada* had drawn miles ahead. When the white hull of the larger boat had been smudged by distance and was half-way below the horizon, I gave up sailing and cranked the hated engine.

It was not difficult for me to dislike the engine because I am not at all mechanically-minded and for months it had been playing up. Soon after *Kylie* had got to Mexico the built-in alternator – or rotor, or whatever it was – had stopped charging the battery, and so during the months when we had been in Mexican and Belizean waters the battery had had to be lifted out and ferried to *Nada* for recharging when opportunity offered – about once every ten days. In theory, these rechargings allowed me to use the cabin lights for a few hours a week but my anxiety to keep enough battery power in hand to start the engine in emergencies had driven me to near-abstinence.

So far, there had been few emergencies, and anchoring, weighing and manoeuvring in restricted coral waters under sail had not overtaxed me in the moderate trade-wind weather, and the anchorages themselves had been so far from being crowded that on several days while cruising the barrier reef of Belize we had not seen any other boats, let alone got close enough to be in danger of collision. It had helped me, too, that most of *Kylie*'s courses from the Yucatán southward to Guatemala had lain across the wind or directly to leeward.

So far, then, the most common reason for using the engine and its gearbox had been to re-float the boat after running aground. Ground-ings had happened quite often – between the Stuart and Snake Cays as many as three a day – but had happened more often to *Nada* than to *Kylie*, partly because the Calders' boat draws six feet while mine draws only four foot four, but mainly because Nigel was determined that his cruising guide would give reliable information about soundings. He is a stickler for accuracy, and so was taking great pains to explore every nook and cranny his readers might be tempted to go into. Given that many soundings on the charts we were using had not been updated since Queen Victoria was on the throne, these groundings were only to be expected. Usually I was able to re-float *Kylie* by laying out a small anchor and winching her off the shoal, but sometimes I speeded up the proceedings by using the engine, cranking it by hand to save electricity. Nigel had said that the engine fault lay somewhere deep inside its vitals, and that repairing it would mean a complete dismantling. My intention was to cruise Lago Izabal and the Bay Islands, and then go back to the Rio Dulce and have the engine repaired, using the spare parts which I'd brought out from Britain.

For an hour *Kylie* puttered westward, her bows making a continuous ripple which scarcely broke. Five miles away on either hand, the jungle was a waxy smear. In the shade of the cockpit awning I drank canned lager and smoked my pipe, now and then glancing astern, looking for wind.

4
Three Reefs and One Extra

It came from the east, at first barely strong enough to nudge aside the wraith of pipe smoke which hung between the backstays above my head. I cut the engine and poled out the ghoster. After a couple of weak lollops the sail caught the wind and bulged, and soon *Kylie* was making three knots down the length of the lake again, towards Puerto Refugio.

Puerto Refugio lived up to only half of its promises. It was a safe haven from the prevailing wind, which by the time *Kylie* reached it was blowing twenty knots and raising three-foot waves, but as a port it did poorly. I rounded a long bill of land with expectations of seeing a rough-and-ready warehouse or – at the very least – a primitive jetty, but before me lay nothing but miles of silent water and brooding jungle. In spite of the bright sunshine Puerto Refugio looked altogether dull. I hung the mosquito net across the companionway and took myself below.

Perhaps the dullness lay not in the surroundings but in their beholder, for months later Nigel was to describe the area as "lovely", and before long I too came to think of the area as being not at all bad. My change of mind began when we came across the nests of *Gymnostinops montezuma*, a species of weaver bird which had been building at the edge of the jungle. We set eyes on the results of its labours while phut-phutting up the Rio Calochic in *Nada*'s dinghy, eight miles west of Puerto Refugio. Till then we had wound through miles of, to me, uninteresting jungle in which sullen Indians were thwacking bushes with long machetes, or making smoky fires. Neither the vegetation nor the people looked at all remarkable, but eventually some isolated trees between a plantation and the river caught our eye. The trees were sixty to eighty feet tall, with high boughs and slender trunks. From the branches hung half a dozen objects which had the shape of shoulder bags but were the size and texture of the coir fenders used on boats before plastics came in. At their tops, where the fenders' rope-eyes would have been, the bags sagged inwards and, instead of hanging by a single eye, each hung from two long straps. The straps had been woven from the same grassy fibres as the nest itself so that, in fact, the bag and its straps were all of a piece.

We stopped the engine and waited to see what would happen. For minutes, nothing did. The dinghy lay stationary on the dark river and above us the leaves of the trees lifted to the wind, but the nests hung unvisited. Nigel half-turned in the sternsheets to re-start the motor.

"Hold on!" whispered Terrie, pointing. A dozen small dark birds had fluttered out from the jungle and were clinging to the underside of the bags. As many as four attached themselves to some bags, but others attracted none.

"Watch, children!" commanded Terrie.

The birds clung to the bags for an instant, then disappeared inside them.

"Ah!" went I on seeing this. Having thought of the nests as being bags, I had expected the birds to go in through an opening in the top but they hadn't – they'd disappeared through the sides and bottom.

After that, delights came thickly. In another river west of the Palochic, hyacinths clustered about the boat, blushing pinkly as Nigel focused his camera on them. From El Estor on the northern shore of the lake we jolted in a station wagon over rough roads to the Boqueron Canyon, where we paddled canoes up a gorge which became so overcast and oppressive that I felt like saying an Our Father. Then, too quickly for me after the solemn silence, we hung between boulders, roaring and kicking, suspended from ropes in rushing white water, until I contracted a splitting headache. By this time the pell-mell activity had become too much, so when, while polishing his glasses at the end of the day, Nigel invited me to accompany the Calder family on a visit to Finca El Paraiso, Paradise Farm, and afterwards trek miles uphill in torrid heat so as to inspect a boiling-hot waterfall, I cried off, saying I would go for a quiet sail on the lake instead, and meet them afterwards at El Estor.

Setting the genoa, not perhaps hearing but certainly feeling its hanks whirr up the forestay, heaving hard on the tack tackle till the luff creased, and making up the fall of the halyard will give me a great deal of pleasure, I thought, and so it did. *Kylie* stole out of a south-western bay of the lake an hour after sunrise on a morning which carried promises of a quiet but pleasant sail. Cloud lay in the valleys and although the wind was blowing only very lightly from the south-west, it was enough to fill the ghoster. I lit a pipe and settled down. In an

Weaver birds and nest.

hour or two the breeze would fade entirely but by then *Kylie* would have made eight miles of easting and be in the middle of the lake. There, after a period of calm during which I would perhaps play my harmonica and inspect a floating hyacinth or two, the trade wind would filter in from the Bahia de Amatique and waft me back to the undemanding anchorage at Puerto Refugio for a lukewarm beer and an afternoon nap . . .

Before *Kylie* could reach the middle of the lake the wind veered ten degrees and strengthened, and the mountain tops were shawled grey. I reefed the main, set the smaller genoa and steered for El Estor, thinking that its barge basin would give shelter if the wind got up further. A mile from the town its pastel walls were dulled by rain and the lake between *Kylie* and the shore was suddenly poppled thickly with whitecaps. Barge basin or not, El Estor had become a place into which a sailing boat could not easily get. I handed the genoa, tied a second row of reefs in the mainsail, lay hove-to and waited for the squall to blow itself out.

By the time at which the trade wind should have been building from the east, the westerly wind was still blowing strongly and the mountains had become heavily clouded, squatting down low in the dark landscape like protesters do in England while pulling their jerseys over their knees against the cold. I too was feeling a bit chilly. Wearing my Winter North Atlantic outfit, I held the tiller a-weather, scudding seventy degrees to the waves, looking for shore markers but not seeing them. At two o'clock the wind veered to west-north-west and blew five knots stronger, so I deep-reefed the main, set a small jibsail, lay hove-to again and put the kettle on.

By half-past four the daylight was so weak that the red and green harbour lights of Mariscos were switched on. From two miles offshore they looked very tempting but I did not steer towards them. Mariscos is the only port on the southern shore of Lago Izabal but, apart from the fact that a white-hulled ferry to El Estor came out of it twice daily, I knew nothing about its harbour and, in any case, it lay on a dangerous lee shore. Letting draw the jib, I headed northwards for the opposite bank of the lake, some eight miles distant.

Though Guatemala is a richly interesting country, obtaining up-to-date facts about its history and geography can be difficult. No one can say how many thousand people have been killed in the civil war which has been going on there for sixty years, and the government keeps even the most basic geographical information to itself. Detailed maps of the country were not on sale to the public on the grounds that they could fall into the hands of the revolutionary guerrillas. Not possessing any map of Lago Izabal of more recent date or larger size than those which George Philips might have published in a Latin-American version of his atlas, I could therefore only guess at what I might find on the north shore of the lake when I got there.

Heeling to thirty-knot gusts, under the small jib and deeply reefed mainsail *Kylie* beat northward, fifty degrees to the wind, flurries of spray and rain dashing hard against the coachroof. At dusk the wind was as strong as ever but the waves were going down in size. I judged from this that the shore might be only a mile or two distant but there was no way of knowing this for certain. Even if I switched it on, the satnav's data would not tally reliably with my ancient chart, nor could soundings give me a usefully approximate position-line, for the lake had shoaled only five feet in the course of an hour. The sight of shore lights would have been helpful, but none was piercing the gloom from the north – or from any other sector of the compass, come to that.

By seven-thirty the depthsounder was showing twenty feet and the waves were no more than three feet from trough to crest. I backed the jib, stood on the coachroof and peered about, looking for any slight variation in the texture of the gloom which might give me a hint of where the shore was. A hand's span to weather of the jib leech there appeared a faint white glow. I let draw the sail and steered cautiously towards it.

Perhaps I have got less out of reading the poetry of Betjeman than I ought, but white shore-lights which are not navigation marks always seem to tinge their beams with amber, a colour which raises thoughts of angel cakes and buttered toast. When looked at more closely through flurries of rain however, this particular glow turned out to be stark white. It was not a shore light but the anchor light of a ketch. By the height of its mizzen mast and the glimmer of a faintly gleaming bowsprit, I knew it could only be *Nada*. Had I arrived willy-nilly at Paradise Farm and, conceivably, buttered toast? If so, where were its ambery lights? The shore was hidden in darkness and, apart from its anchor light, the boat was dark too, with not a chink coming from the cabin. At barely nine at night, this was odd. I handed the jib and let go the anchor.

How was it, I wondered, that at the end of a day which had begun with our heading off in different directions onto a 250-square-mile lake we had finished up only yards apart? And why had the Calders gone to bed so early? I would have liked to have asked them these questions straight away but I didn't. With ears like mine, asking questions in the dark always brings about more perplexity than was there before I asked them.

After a restless night at anchor I picked up the walkie-talkie at six in the morning, fiddled with its squelch knob and asked Terrie what on earth the Calders were up to.

"This isn't Terrie, it's Nigel!" replied a voice which crackled with what I hoped was nothing but squelch. "Terrie and the children are still at the *finca* and I'm going in there now to pick them up."

Soon he had weighed anchor and was steering for a small bay, on

Nada goes adrift.

the shores of which, presumably, lay the *finca*. The wind by now had fallen to fifteen knots but the sky was still unappealing and so I stayed below and made myself a half-pint of porridge.

Minutes later, leaning overboard to wash the pan, I was surprised to see that *Nada* was still in view, immobile in the centre of the bay, listing to starboard, hard aground near a small pole. I cranked the engine and motored towards her to give help, but before *Kylie* could get close two large motorized *cayucos* had sped out from the shore and their crews were laying out a kedge anchor.

Nigel backed the warp to his electric windlass and heaved taut but *Nada* did not budge. Water boiled at the stern as her propeller thrust alternately ahead and astern, but still she didn't move. The next thing was, Nigel had set the headsails, the mainsail and the mizzen, hove taut the sheets and was cleating them. With the wind pressing on her sails, *Nada* heeled fifteen degrees, reducing her draught by a few vital inches. The *cayucos* buzzed about, laying out a second anchor. After more hauling on warps and thumping from the engine, in half an hour *Nada* was freed. Soon afterwards Terrie and the children were safely aboard and our two boats were making back towards the Castillo San Felipe where, anchored off it that evening, we drank tea and swapped notes.

It seemed that the wind had blown more suddenly and strongly on the north shore of the lake than at its centre. Having anchored *Nada* in seventeen feet of water two hundred yards off the *finca*, the family had walked into the foothills, had bathed in the hot waterfall and were making their way back to the boat when the branches above their heads were thrown into turmoil by a sudden gust. Fearful for the safety of his boat, Nigel ran down the hillside towards the bay, then hidden from view by the jungle, leaving Terrie and the children to follow. A youth from the *finca* raced up the path from the bay, crying that the yacht had broken adrift. By the time Nigel got to the dinghy, *Nada* was a mile away, dragging her anchor southwards in the storm.

Trying to reach the drifting yacht by dinghy would have been suicidal, so at a shout from a fisherman Nigel jumped into a large *cayuco*. Two miles offshore *Nada* was drifting sideways, broadside to the gale, her bow constrained by the dragging anchor but making one mile an hour through the water and heeling so far to leeward that the sidedeck was awash. The first attempt to board her by ranging the *cayuco* alongside was a failure, and when, during a second attempt, the fisherman's head was near-missed by the plunging bobstay, a different approach was tried. The fisherman manoeuvred the *cayuco* so that it was at right angles to *Nada*'s hull and then drove forward at speed. The rough-hewn bow smashed through the waves, tore a hole in the safety netting and crunched onto *Nada*'s foredeck. Nigel leapt onto the deck and the *cayuco* backed off.

This had happened in late afternoon, when *Kylie* had been off Mariscos. Later, while I had been beating northwards in winds which had rarely gusted at more than thirty knots, Nigel had had to battle against a whole gale. Even with her powerful engine, *Nada* had been unable to get back to the *finca* before night fell, and so he had anchored off the eastern headland of the bay and turned in.

"It was pretty lucky that you anchored when and where you did," I felt like telling him, "otherwise you might have run onto that pile of rocks in the middle of the night."

Running onto a pile of rocks at any time was bad enough, but the idea of its happening in the dark was dreadful. To dissolve this unappealing vision I raised my eyes above the rim of my mug and said:

"I say, Nigel, is there any tea left in the pot?"

As we were to learn later though, the horror of running onto rocks in darkness was to happen.

5

Selling a Shotgun

I made for the sea, stealing eastward onto the river at daybreak, but the
puny airs from the west lived barely an hour, dwindled by the sun. The
Rio Dulce seemed lifeless too, with not a hyacinth nor fish seen. I
handed the ghoster and swung the starting-handle, grudging the need
to get into the gorge before headwinds could rush down the mountains.
Abeam of the Rio Chacon Machaca the halyards slapped the mast in a
wind that came too soon. I would like to be able to say I sailed into that
wind, but time seemed short that day, for I wanted to get to Livingston
at the river mouth and hurry on to the Bay Islands to meet up with the
Calders.

Throttle two-thirds open, *Kylie* motored into the gorge. Glassy water
reflected pelicans, and snow-white egrets in trees. Cormorants whirred
past grave Indians who paddled their boats kneeling, feet tucked neatly
under thighs. All except one boat were *cayucos*, ancient even before
Columbus came. This other was a twentieth-century dory carrying
swatches of dyed cotton, tee-shirts, flip-flops and combs. Two stout
women wearing wide straw hats above knotted headscarves paddled it
from door to door, showing and selling their wares.

Tall and sheer – but not nearly so grey or grim – as Suffolk castles,
the canyon walls cast deep shadows. A headless creature the colour of
an earthworm but half a metre wide wallowed past below the surface
on the darker side of the boat. It could have been the remains of a
gigantic snake, a manatee, an alligator belly-upwards, or the torso of a
corpse. The sight of a corpse floating down the Rio Dulce was not a
rarity, a body having been pulled out of the water the week before I
left. At Mario's they said it had been found among water hyacinths
with a bullet hole in it.

"D'you want to buy my shotgun?" I asked the port captain in a long-
delayed reaction to that incident when I got to Livingston.

"What are you asking for it?" he replied in English, a language
understood there by few and spoken by hardly any.

"Two hundred and fifty quetzales." (£44 or $70.60).

I had deposited the gun with him on first coming into Guatemala and
now it lay on his desk, ready to be signed out for the Bay Islands of

Honduras. I had bought it three years previously in a market town in Suffolk, after hearing stories about the murders of yacht crews by pirates.

"The worst area is the China Sea; they come at you in boatloads," had said a mariner who'd seen them doing it; "but the Caribbean can be bad too."

Having mulled over this news I had hitched a lift to Beccles and bought a twelve-bore shotgun, though not without one or two misgivings, for I had scarcely ever touched a firearm, let alone fired one. By way of practice I had it let off at an empty baked-beans can in mid-Atlantic, but so far I had not been set upon by pirates. Indeed, the gun had seemed to stir up as much hostility in the forces of the law as it was ever likely to meet from pirates. My difficulties had begun soon after I walked off a flight at Palma de Majorca airport, where I had been pounced on by a bullet-headed policeman and given a fierce grilling. He growled that the shotgun had been flown out from England in an unlawful manner, travelling in the cargo hold instead of in the pilot's cabin where the regulations said it should have been. Till the Gatwick handlers confessed to him over the phone that they had disregarded the stowage rules, I was held as a suspected terrorist, incommunicado and fuming. Later in the same year, merely transporting the weapon from Turkey to Greece and back again in *Kylie* had given rise to flurries of baleful questions from rival officials and brief but off-putting detentions in both their camps. Getting the shotgun into and out of countries in the New World had not been quite as stressful as doing the same in the Mediterranean basin had been but, always and everywhere, just having the gun had meant conflict and delay. By now I'd had quite enough of it; the gun had got to go.

"Two hundred and twenty-five," I said to the port captain, a dapper *teniente* in the Guatemalan navy who was nearing the end of a period of harbour duty at Livingston and not hankering to get afloat again. It was not difficult to see why. His office stood on a prime site, a cliff overlooking the sparkling Bahia de Amatique. Fanned by a cooling trade wind and attended by lackeys whose cream khaki uniforms were almost as neatly pressed as his was, the port captain had a cushy job. Certainly his present workplace was more colourful and roomy than any he would be given aboard Guatemalan warships, all of which are on the small side and painted a murky grey.

"Two hundred and twenty quetzales I will give you," he said, firmly re-fastening the leather strap of his gold wristwatch. Outside his office two subordinates were painting a shoulder-high wall in a terra-cotta shade of pink seen more often in England than elsewhere. Was it, I wondered, a sign of repressed Anglophilia? His government had broken off diplomatic relations with our government in 1963 and so far had showed no signs of mending them. Perhaps he was a frustrated diplomat rehearsing a hoped-for career as a naval attaché in London, where even his boot-cupboard might be painted pink.

"All right, then," I conceded; "two-twenty."

Half of the quetzales went on rum, sold by a hollow-cheeked storekeeper whose daughter smiled inquiringly at me when I went into his shop but who was then shooed out of my sight before I could say "*Buenas días*".

"I forbid my child to learn English," said the storekeeper to my dismay. "Life here is very hard, you must understand; learning English would make her want riches that are not possible for us to get. For people like us, knowing English only makes life more terrible than it already is."

What reasons he had for thinking that a customer clutching a Spanish phrase-book would beguile his daughter in English was not a question worth going into. I would have liked to have argued against his anti-English attitude, but how could I sincerely do this when I had just spent more quetzales on a week's tipple than a Guatemalan in a *cayuco* could earn in a month?

By seven the next morning *Kylie* had left the Rio Dulce and I was at sea again for the first time in months, listening to fluent Caribbean English from Radio Belize, whose views of local conditions were more uplifting. The wind, it said in particular, would be between east and north-east at ten to fifteen knots.

Under the large genoa *Kylie* sailed thirty-five miles in seven hours, from Livingston to the Sapodilla Cays, anchoring at three in the afternoon on white sand covered by eel grass. I drank a little rum and looked at the chart.

My plan was to head north-eastward from the cays soon after daybreak, holding that course for as long as the night breeze would last. When the trade wind set in to replace it at noon I hoped to be able to sail close-hauled to the nearest of the Bay Islands, seventy-six miles distant.

Light south-westerly airs carried me through the channel between Hunting Cay and a smaller palm island to the south. Soon the greeny-white shallows of the Sapodilla Cays lay astern and *Kylie* was heading north-east in dark blue water hundreds of feet deep while her skipper gazed at the shadow of his own head, which the reflected sun had encircled with a glittering corona as worn by high-ranking saints like – to bring in a famous one – St Francis of Assisi. Into this picture, half a boat's-length from the halo and being slowly overtaken, paddled a hawksbill turtle, travelling in the same direction but making only half a knot to *Kylie*'s two. Like *Kylie*, it was listing slightly, encumbered by a crust of barnacles which had colonised the starboard lower platelets of its shell. The turtle paddled gamely through the water, its forelegs bent backwards by genetic chemistry and long swims. As *Kylie* drew abeam, it stopped paddling, peered at me and blinked. We looked at each other with what in the turtle seemed to be – and in me was certainly – a gleam of interest, for plainly in many ways our cases were alike. Both of us had come into the world during the hours of darkness and in spite of – or, perhaps, because of – huge odds stacked against our seeing the next sunrise, had headed for the sea as soon as we possibly could.

Curious but not gossipy, given to shedding a tear or two at family partings, solitary but not lonely, eyeing land with interest but wary of setting foot on it because of the bother we might encounter, were other traits we shared. Both of us had spent some years (about seven in the turtle's case; in mine, six) travelling the same ocean in once-shiny carapaces that were forever being fouled by barnacles. Somewhere back along the line we may have shared genes, too.

The creature half-shut both eyes, extended its neck and opened its mouth a fraction, as if stifling a yawn, or – just possibly – a groan. I wondered whether St Francis would have blessed its barnacles or crushed them.

The turtle closed its mouth and lowered its head. I had the pleasing thought that I could be looking at a turtle which no other person had ever seen. Another pleasure was knowing that the turtle hadn't paddled off in alarm. It lay in the water, neck partly extended and head cocked sideways. Before I could make a start on scraping off its barnacles, *Kylie* had carried me out of arm's reach. I watched the creature drift astern, tituping slightly in the waves. It seemed a pity that it hadn't given voice.

At noon the wind fell to a whisper, then veered through north and north-east before settling at east-by-north and building to ten knots. *Kylie* beat south-eastward, making four-plus knots through the water but, on account of current and leeway, only 2.2 miles an hour towards her goal. I set the wind-vane steering gear and went below to tighten up the dividers and plot an estimated position.

Seven hours close hauled on the port tack brought me to five miles of the Honduran mainland, so I went about, hoping that another seven hours on starboard tack would at dawn raise Utila, the first of the Bay Islands, but after midnight the wind died away to nothing. I handed sail, cranked the engine and motored in the direction of invisible Utila.

Owing to a slip-up by the late George Philips, I knew less about the Bay Islands than any other places that I had so far visited; in fact, until Nigel mentioned them six months previously I didn't know that they existed. I cannot have been the only person to have been in the dark; perhaps Dod Orsborne hadn't known of them either. The 1:15,000,000 maps on pages 90–91 of the *New Modern School Atlas* would have helped him to navigate *Girl Pat* to all the other archipelagos of Central America and the West Indies if he had wanted to, but, somehow or other, the Bay Islands had been missed off. So far as most British schoolchildren – or ship-stealers – could see, the area of the Gulf of Honduras between Puerto Cortez and Trujillo contained nothing but water. Not until fifty-one years after Philips' thirty-third atlas had come out did I discover that the Admiralty knew differently.

On the Admiralty chart, the far south-western approaches to the Bay Islands seemed free of dangers to small boats like *Kylie*. Here and there, the Admiralty recorded shoals, some labelled "PA" (Position Approximate) or "PD" (Position Doubtful), but all except the Salmedina were shown as having ample water above them. Nevertheless, "Dangerous uncharted shoals are likely to be encountered anywhere", had written the Hydrographer, so from time to time I switched on the depthsounder to check.

The night seemed long but, at last, four o'clock came, traditionally in *Kylie* the time for a choc-bar and a snifter to mark the ending of the graveyard watch. I sipped a finger of rum and wrote up the log: "Midnight: Course steered 100°. Error 3°E. Distance Made Good 54'. Wind E x N, force 1. Engine on again." A few minutes after four I stopped the motor and re-set the genoa to light airs which were creeping in from the north. At four-fifteen the blips on the depthsounder flickered from fifteen fathoms to four and stayed there. I corked the bottle, clambered to the cockpit, unlatched the wind-vane, cast off the tiller yoke-lines and backed the headsail. To the north-east, where the fifteen-mile light on Utila should have been winking but, so far as I could see, wasn't, heavy black cloud was back-lit by a pearly

41

dawn. Twenty miles to the south, Mayan gods were throwing fireworks at an 8000-foot mountain. The flashes shimmered on the wave-tops but did nothing to illuminate the depth. I dug out the hand-lead and cast it. The line ran out till a single strip of leather was between finger and thumb: five fathoms. The depthsounder had been right: the water was shallower than the chart said.

With the headsail aback and the helm a-lee, *Kylie* lay quietly, making a quarter of a knot through the water. I started up the satnav, fed it an estimated position and waited for it to tell me exactly where I was, sleepily thinking meanwhile how agreeable it would be to inform Nigel Calder and Her Majesty's Hydrographer that *Kylie* had come across a $4^1/_2$-fathom shoal at latitude precisely so-and-so, longitude exactly such-and-such; but, though I lay hove-to for half an hour and gorged the satnav with half a dozen encouraging tit-bits, all it came up with was "NO FIX". I pencilled an estimated position on the chart and wrote "$4^1/_2$ (PA)" next to it.

One fact I did know for certain, having looked it up in an almanac in case of having to take a star sight, was that for me and everyone else at sea on my estimated parallel of latitude the sun would rise at 0518 hours by Ship's Mean Time, twenty-seven minutes after Civil Twilight had officially begun. Pumpkin Hill, a hump on what I took to be Utila, had become vaguely visible some minutes before, during Nautical Twilight, while I had been waiting in vain for the satnav to tell me where I was. Pumpkin Hill's coming into view was accompanied by a ripple of noise from the mainland. This might have happened because the archaeologists from Chicago had at last ended their tour of Mayan temples and were giving their guides a hearty handclap. It could, on the other hand, have been thunder.

The sun came up. *Kylie* sailed on towards the island. At first it looked to me much as it must have looked to every other European who had so far seen it, from Pinzó and de Solis in the early sixteen hundreds, continuing through the seventeenth century with buccaneers such as Morgan and going on to surveyors like Commander Owen, RN, who in 1835 had characterised it as being "low, swampy and thickly wooded", with a peak at its eastern end. The words "Oyster beds" written across a lagoon, and his drawing-in of a path showed that the six-mile-long island had had a number of people dwelling on it at the time, but there cannot have been very many because the path shown on the chart was barely three hundred yards long and anyone using it would have run into a colossal bush. And even the word "Inhabited"

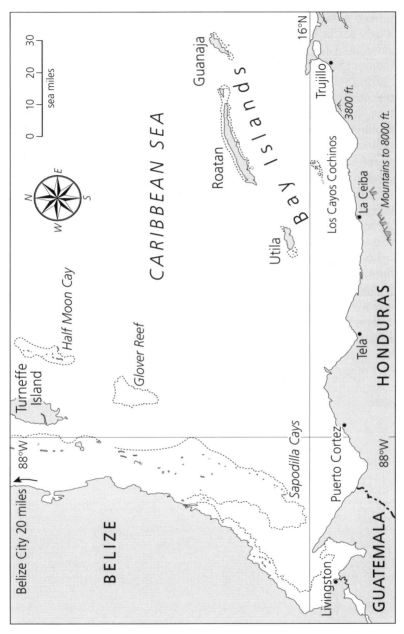

Chart 2: Caribbean Sea: Rio Dulce to the Bay Islands of Honduras.

printed alongside Suck-Suck Cay off the south-western end of Utila would not have led a nineteenth-century mariner to think of finding any substantial dwellings there, for Suck-Suck was only an eighth of a mile long, no bigger than scores of other islets in the archipelagos of the north-west Caribbean. "Inhabited" written alongside so small an island meant only that the mariner could look forward to beholding no more than half a dozen grass huts and a *cayuco* or two. Heading for the cay a century and a half after Commander Owen had charted it, I thought it more than likely that any dwellings would have long since gone.

But from four miles away it was plain that Suck-Suck was being dwelt on still. Instead of a straggle of grass huts however, I was looking at an orderly array of solid buildings whose fronts were painted in bold colours and, in place of a small dugout canoe drawn up on the beach, a fifty-ton motor fishing-vessel anchored off it. The fishing-vessel had two masts and a single funnel, just like *Girl Pat*.

I rubbed salt from my eyes and picked up the binoculars. No wonder the satnav had said "NO FIX". During the long watches of the night it had become as forgetful of small Caribbean islands as George Philips and was now leading me seriously astray.

Before me stood a trim row of East Anglian beach huts. Somehow, I was sailing into Southwold again.

6

Up, Down and English

With the wind abaft the beam *Kylie* reached through a fifty-yard channel between two gingerbread-brown reefs, hooked up into the wind and anchored in forty feet of water abreast of the trawler. Low and swampy most of Utila may be, but looked at from *Kylie*'s cockpit the south-western end of the island was decidedly hilly, with patchy green woodland and rust-coloured earth sloping down quite steeply from the north before stretching westward a couple of miles and tailing off into the sea in a dark blur, with no signs of human habitation anywhere.

The southern aspect of the anchorage, though, was nothing but houses. Though each house was separate from its neighbour, no chink of sky was visible between them, being blocked out by other dwellings close behind. With no background landscape to give a sense of depth, the houses looked like pop-ups in children's story books, ready to collapse at the turn of a page.

Spanish phrase-book in my rucksack, I rowed towards a short jetty, glancing over my shoulder as I went. The houses seemed to hobble out to meet me, clustering into the water on stilts.

I made fast the dinghy painter near where two small girls were sitting in shadow on a flight of wooden steps which led to the open doorway of a dark green house.

"*Como?*" I said, trying out a form of greeting which I thought I had heard Terrie use in Mexico and Guatemala. A girl lifted her head, pulled aside a light brown curl and looked at me blankly.

"*Buenas días,*" I said.

She parted her lips but looked down again without speaking.

A raised concrete pathway led me past small gardens enclosed by knee-high chicken-wire fences and bright yellow flowers trailing from white-painted cans onto gravelly ground. A young man wearing khaki shorts, a blue singlet and a baseball cap overtook me, carrying a ten-foot plank.

"*Buenas días*," I said again as he drew level, but he too didn't speak.

Soon after these unpromising encounters I met a woman named Daphne Howell and discovered why my Spanish had fallen flat. Dressed in a fawn skirt and a sensible but not frumpish blouse, Mrs Howell was running one of the island's two shops. She spoke softly but urgently, in English which seemed at times to hark back to the Norfolk-Suffolk border. I bought a bottle of merry-looking fizz and bent forward to catch what she was saying.

Four generations before Commander Owen had labelled Suck-Suck as being lived on, she said, Utila and the larger Bay Islands of Roatan and Guanaja had already been settled by people of British stock, many of them logwood-cutters from the Honduran mainland but also sailors, including (with a sideways nod at the trawler) pirates who'd preyed on the Spanish treasure fleets. These Bay Islanders of old had behaved so awkwardly towards the conquistadors that the government in London had said that it was only fair and right that the islands should become parts of the British Empire . . .

She broke off to hand out glossy sweetmeats to three grey-eyed children who were looking me over from the doorway.

". . . and all of us talk only English," put in a white-haired woman in a flowery pinafore who had come in to buy flour; "and those of us as can talk Spanish, won't."

"Hello!" I then said to the children, but they shied away, and when I asked the white-haired woman to tell me more, her hands fluttered to her cheeks and she turned away from me as well.

"Oh, you see, Aunt Olive has her baking to do," explained Daphne, "but you can surely call on her by and by, I guess."

"What time would that be?" I said, glancing at my watch.

"Oh . . . just by and by. . .," she said.

Tippling merrily, I walked the remaining yards of Suck-Suck and crossed a narrow boardwalk to its neighbouring cay, Pigeon. Though even smaller in area than Suck-Suck, Pigeon was built up just as densely with clapboard houses, and except for half a dozen *mestizos* gazing into a dismembered engine at the water's edge near the board-walk, the people there had the same pale brown hair and were speaking only English.

"Gerroff!" for instance, cried a boy of about fourteen while being knelt on by the young man in a baseball cap who had set down his plank against a maroon-red house and was now tugging at the youngster's bat.

"You were catched, Our Jack!" cried the young man, wrenching the
bat away from the 14-year-old and handing it to a girl so that she could
carry on with the ball game which they were playing on a few square
yards of unbuilt-on grass.

"In 1959," put in a grey-haired man who said his name was Hulbert,
"the government sent over some policemen to make us celebrate the
hundredth anniversary of the ending of British rule."

"What happened, Hulbert?"

" 'Hulbert' . . .? It's 'Albert', not 'Hulbert'."

I turned my earpiece up to level 4. "Sorry, Albert, I was on low
power."

"Somehow," he said, nodding towards the plank, "the lot of them fell
into the sea . . ."

Since then the Honduran government had set about punishing the
Bay Islanders, went on Albert gruffly, while showing me a generator
and an ice-making plant on the downwind end of Pigeon. Apart from
the concrete pathway that we were standing on, the government
in Tegucigalpa had funded nothing, not even a teacher of English, he
said.

We turned about and walked back to Suck-Suck against the trade
wind blowing lengthways down the islands. On the bridge, my hearing
aid started whistling. Albert turned his back to the wind and worked
his mouth. Between whistles, I heard: "We don't . . . clep our cays
Suck-Suck and Pigeon . . . to us they're Up and Down . . ."

A rather formal Aunt Olive came to the door of her house when I
tapped my knuckles on it. She'd taken off the pinafore, changed into a
darker dress and combed her hair into the 1950s *Woman's Weekly* style
which my mother used to wear when she was expecting a visit from
the landlord. Having sat me down in a sturdy wooden armchair, Aunt
Olive backed away with a series of bobs and nods, then took up the
grievance about education where Albert had left off.

"Time and over we ask the government to teach English reading and
writing in school, but they won't . . ."

"Well," I heard myself saying, knowing that Honduras was the
poorest of the Central American states and sixty per cent of its
population were illiterate, "teaching English might seem to be a bit of
a luxury when so many people can't even read or write Spanish . . ."

"*Luxury* . . .?" she said stiffly. "When Queen Victoria gave us away
to Honduras it was a let-down. We were so angered that we got out the
arquebuses . . ." She crossed her hands in her lap and stuck out her chin.

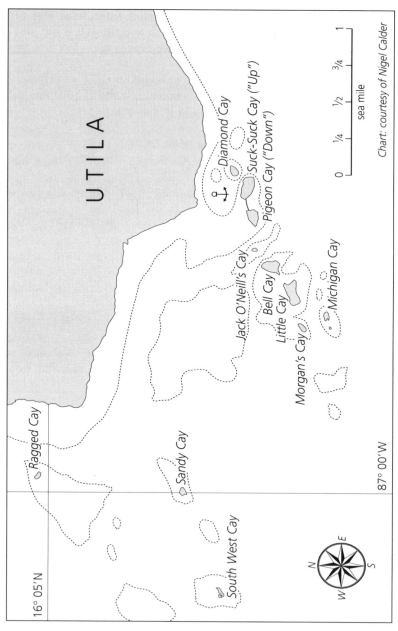

Chart 3: Gulf of Honduras: South-west Utila and adjacent cays.

" . . . so now we're teaching the children how to read and write English ourselves, after school . . ."

"*Arquebuses* . . .?" I wanted to ask her, but now she was looking down at the floorboards and shaking her head.

". . . but oh, dear," she went on, knuckling her chin, "the lessons aren't coming along as well as they might. At Michaelmas we'd a class of eight, but now we're down to four . . .." The hands flew together and clasped each other. She and Daphne were using books the minister had left with them before he'd stopped coming, and though they were sensible reading, the children thought of them as being a mite old-fashioned . . .. Most of the books were lodged in the church or at Daphne's, not here at hers, though she could lay hands on one to show me if I wanted . . .. But, dearie me, no, the children weren't coming on at all . . .

From a wooden chest in a corner she took out a copy of *Alice's Adventures in Wonderland*. It had been printed in 1901, the year the old Queen had died. The limp oilcloth cover was so dark with age and use that I had to hold it at an angle to the light so as to make out the title.

While she was in the kitchen cutting me a slice of carrot cake I thumbed through it:

> *"That's the reason they're called lessons," the Gryphon remarked: "because they lessen from day to day."*

"D'you think," she said as I picked up my hat, "that there's any chance of the Queen taking us back again . . .?"

I rowed back to *Kylie* with the sun in my eyes, dazzled. Pretending to discover islands where George Philips had shown only sea had been a fanciful amusement, something done over a rum and a sweet biscuit at the end of the graveyard watch. Not seeing the light on Utila had darkened the mystery but had made it no less fanciful; one which, in the normal way, I would have forgotten by noon. Then the Southwold beach huts had risen from the sea, along with the *Girl Pat*, and so I had kidded myself that I was sailing towards an England as it used to be in, at the latest, the Twenties or Thirties. The shape and style of the dwellings told me that my fancy had been nearer to the truth of the matter than not: Up and Down could be taken as little bits of 1920 England all right, but after talking to Aunt Olive it seemed that the language timeframe was centuries out of joint. Except for their stilts, the houses had looked no different from wooden houses still to be

". . . We got out the arquebuses"

found on the coasts of Essex and Suffolk. But since the earliest logwood-cutters had built their first dwellings and the buccaneers had stopped harrying galleons, flintlocks had come and gone and barrels had been rifled. We were almost into the twenty-first century, yet here on Up and Down the people were still talking about using arquebuses, a sort of weaponry which even Sir Henry Morgan in the 1680s might have thought of as being a trifle antique . . .

An hour before sunset the young man in the baseball cap chuntered out in a diesel-engined dory, boarded the trawler and disappeared into its wheelhouse. I went below and poured a rum, returning with it to the cockpit to watch the bird-flights and the changing sky. I noticed that the young man was now standing in the trawler's bows, gazing across fifty yards of water at *Kylie*.

"Haven't I met you somewhere before," I thought, "wearing a different hat . . . ?"

. . . in 1946 in a diner near the Kill Van Kull he had been a homeless Lithuanian in a peakless hat who wanted to know how to spell "possesses", but three years later in Singapore his English had come on so well that he was reading *Angel Pavement* in only two days so as to return it before my ship cleared for Balik Papan and his for Hong Kong.

When we encountered each other again in Mombasa in 1950 he was a bare-headed colonist from the Seychelles, working as a deckhand in the brig *Diolinda*, whose Master was named – incredibly – Captain Hook. By that time, however, he had forgotten all about the Priestley novel and that "possesses" has five s's . . .

When the lower limb of the sun was searing the roofs of Up and Down the man in the baseball cap came down from the trawler and started the dory's engine. I thought he would motor back ashore then, but he steered towards *Kylie* and lay his boat parallel.

"How does that work?" he said, pointing at the wind-vane steering gear.

"Pass me your painter and I'll show you."

Showing and telling him about *Kylie*'s gear was not difficult, but when he asked where my home was and I wrote "Southwold" and "Suffolk" he looked blank.

He ferried me ashore after sunset and I went straight to Aunt Olive's house.

"I'm sailing tomorrow at seven," I told her, "but I'll be coming back here before long."

"Ah?" she said, the lamplight shining through her white hair.

"Keep the class going; I'll get you some more books."

"Will you, then?" she said.

"Yes, of course."

"Would you like some more carrot cake?"

I didn't leave the anchorage at the time I'd said. The seabed was thick mud and foul with old wire hawsers, and so it was nearly eight o'clock before I had weighed anchor and bucketed the mud from the deck. The mud was darker than Suffolk mud but no less sticky.

"English bks for Up & Down," I wrote on my jobs list when *Kylie* was clear of the islands; and added, before the houses sank from sight, " . . . plus atlas."

7

Coxen's Hole to the Settlement

Why her ancestors had settled on a couple of barren coral islets when miles of greener land were to be had on larger islands was not a question I had put to Mrs Howell; nor could an answer to it be found in a despatch from Lieutenant Henry Barnsley, who had served King George II at a time when the first houses were already up on Up and Down.

Roatan, the largest, was " . . . a plentifull Island, Abounding with wild Hoggs," he wrote in 1742, before listing thirteen other species of animals and plants which flourished there, including "Pine Trees of Sufficient Bigness to make Masts and Yards for Merchant Ships". To me, his account seemed to make Roatan a better bet for discerning buccaneers to settle down on than Up and Down were. The island's fifty-mile coastline had an abundance of snug inlets where mariners with piratical leanings could hew and fit masts and stock up with pigs before sailing off to harry Spanish treasure fleets. Now, acres of reddish-brown earth ("Rich and Fertile") rose in hummocks above the bays and coves ("Quantitys of Turtle and Fine Fish") to a skyline on which trees were still plentiful, though most of them looked far too bushy to be made into masts for the size of vessel which Barnsley had had in mind. Bags of room here, I thought, as Roatan rose amply before me, for the first Albert to have hammered up a mansion, exercised an arquebus or hit sixes. Was it cash, curses or carrot cake that had kept him offshore?

Coxen's Hole, the sometime lair of a pirate who chose Roatan, is an inlet on the island's south-western coast. *Kylie* sailed into it late one afternoon and anchored in three fathoms near *Nada*, squeezing onto a narrow underwater shelf between a cay and the town.

A dory muttered up to us, bearing a scowling *mestizo* in uniform.

"Disgraceful!" he said, pointing upwards.

"What's the problem?" Terrie said.

The bands of the Honduran ensigns we were flying underneath our

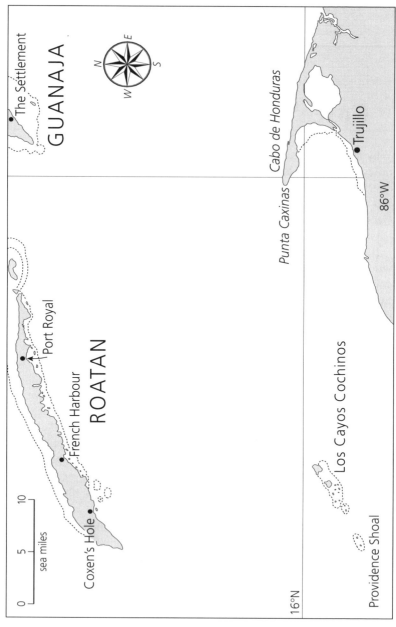

Chart 4: Gulf of Honduras: Roatan and Los Cayos Cochinos.

starboard spreaders were the wrong shade of blue, he replied through his teeth. Indeed, being to his eye so insipidly off-colour as to be almost greens, they were mocking the Republic with every flutter. Nigel outfaced his anger by tut-tutting through his beard, but I hung my head. We had seemed to be cocking a snook at his national pride, and, judging by the beady black looks which he was aiming at us from the dory, painful ructions were about to follow. We dinghied ashore in his wake to be given a formal wigging. By now the sun was wallowing in muddy clouds behind the hillocks and Coxen's Hole was looking grimier by the minute.

But "Ow!" and "Oh!" we cried even before the port captain had begun to needle us about the faulty flags. A species of wildlife which Lieutenant Barnsley made no mention of was attacking us. We hurried into the port captain's office, slapping at our bare legs.

The office was smaller than Aunt Olive's living-room, its walls and ceiling were made of concrete, and dusty screens on its windows cut down the air currents to nil. The port captain seated himself at a desk and glowered at our crew lists, while the adults named in the documents stood before him and sweated. Never one to back away from a shoot-out, Paul held onto his father's hand and glowered back. Pippin behaved more coolly, gliding forward to the desk with a charming smile which had turned Mexican officials into putty.

This one at Coxen's Hole was not so pliable. Only on payment of fifty lempiras (£8.33 or $13.33) would it be possible for flags of an approvable shade of blue to be ready for collection when we reported to his office on the following morning. In the meantime, *Señora y Señores*, affixing an entry visa to our passports would attract a fee of one hundred and forty lempiras (£23.33 or $37.33), not counting the stamps . . ..

"*Mordida*," we muttered to one another as we stomped away from the office through a cloud of whirling wildlife to peer morosely at our visas. The extortion was now blatant: the stamps had been prised off used envelopes and stuck onto the visas with glue.

Nigel and Terrie grimly hoisted *Nada*'s heavy dinghy over the guardrail, secured it to the deck and padlocked the outboard motor before going below and shutting themselves in for the night. It took me only seconds to drape fine-meshed netting over *Kylie*'s companionway and forehatch but a further half an hour of bloody close-quarter work with an Irish linen tea-towel overprinted with a picture of Little Miss Muffet and a gigantic spider before the cabin was empty of mosquitoes.

Their pilfering of our lifeblood did not vex us quite as much as did the *mordida*, the "little bite" at our wallets. Elsewhere in the north-west Caribbean we had not made a fuss about this time-honoured habit, but the port captain's bite had been such a whopper that next morning Nigel hammered out a thunderous letter of protest to the government at Tegucigalpa before weighing anchor at midday and storming out of Coxen's Hole to survey six miles of cays, bays, inlets and reefs, up to and including French Harbour. I had sneaked away earlier, creeping out to escape the mosquitoes and no-see-ums, hoping to find the same steady trade wind that had kept my boat free of insects at Up and Down.

Here in the Gulf of Honduras the winter trades usually blew at about fifteen or twenty knots from ENE, but during the past week the wind had lessened and become tardy, sometimes not coming till early afternoon and building to no more than ten or twelve knots before disappearing with the sun. In musky airs which drifted down from the hummocks, *Kylie* tacked out of Coxen's Hole, past the reef and a spindly light-tower, to head offshore in search of the trade wind, but outside the harbour I found only the same westerly airs. I set the ghoster and let the genoa fall onto the foredeck. Sweat runnelled down my arms and legs as I rigged an awning over the cockpit and sprawled beneath it. On the dot of 1 pm my stomach rumbled.

If Lieutenant Barnsley's stomach had made the same noise when he was lying near-becalmed off Roatan he might have laid aside his quill and called for Boyled Hogg, but what I fancied at that moment were dishes that were much crisper: salads of lettuce, radishes and spring onions, with slices of cold apple pie to follow . . .

Yards of shortcrust pastry which had been baked for twenty-five minutes in a moderate-to-hot oven slid into view between the pulpit and the foremost port-hand stanchion. Larger than Up and Down together, a sheer-sided coral hillock surrounded by deep blue water, the forty-acre shoal rose a hundred feet from the seabed to finish in a plateau just below the surface.

I licked my lips and swallowed. Forty acres of pastry became clingfilmed apple-crumble.

However cloudy or clear is the water in which I am sailing, coming upon a shoal always brings a catch to my throat. In the murky North Sea the evidence might be unspectacular: perhaps a single whitecap breaking on an otherwise calm grey sea, or a lifeless patch in the middle of a popple, or a small eddy. Whether the whitecap turns out to be a fish-jump, or the eddy just a tidal current running into still water, a millisecond after seeing it I make a quick swallow and feel like doing an about-turn.

Coming across a shoal in clear water brings a different tremor to the heart but the same sort of catch to the throat. More often than not the size and nature of the shoal is vividly clear, so I can know at once how shallowly it lies. In the Bay Islands, coral which is ten or twelve feet underwater is the colour of Christmas pudding; at about six to eight feet it looks rather like ginger biscuit or treacle tart, and between that level and the surface it resembles uncooked pastry. Sand and weed go through similar colour-changes as they come nearer to the air. Coral at or above sea-level looks like overdone crumble which has been made with too little butter. With this helpful shade-chart in mind I can sail much closer to the shoal than I would feel like doing if it were hidden by cloudy water, but its sudden shimmer still catches at my throat.

Nada lay fifty yards off the southern wall of the reef, her bowsprit pointing towards Nigel, who was vigorously poling the shallows from his dinghy. I put my head out from the shadow of the awning and waved a greeting to Terrie but she didn't wave back. I was sure she was not being huffy though she'd every reason to be, for I was supposed to be helping her husband, not idling past under a canopy while he laboured away in the broiling sun like a coolie.

The bunt of *Kylie*'s ghoster curved roundly as I hardened the sheet to pass under *Nada*'s stern and across the westerly airs. Terrie however still kept her eyes fixed on Nigel. I upturned my pipe, tapped its bowl against the toe-rail and watched what happened to what fell out. The ash floated but the dottle didn't. Soggy even before they got as far as the water, the tobacco-shreds sank into the depths, unused and unusable . . .

But after all, I said to myself, what earthly use could I be to Nigel just now? Here was I, a mile offshore, thirty fathoms under my keel and the wind barely lifting the ghoster. By the time I had handed sail, bent an extra thirty fathoms of rope onto the warp, cast the 25-lb anchor over the bows, pumped up the dinghy and launched it, and rowed over to help Nigel discover the depths, he would have already finished poling them and be back aboard *Nada*, chugging off at five knots to investigate the next shoal. At the rate at which *Kylie* was presently going, I'd have all my work cut out to reach French Harbour before the sun set. Thinking on this, I tamped half a palmful of St Bruno into the bowl of my pipe and, before lighting it, eased the sheet a full inch. *Kylie* moved south-south-eastward at the rate of a hundred feet a minute.

The trade wind came at 2.40, first crinkling the sea, then ruffling it till it looked like a silk counterpane before ironing. I handed the ghoster and hoisted the large genoa. A winch-pawl clicked, the mast tilted, and soon *Kylie* was making all of two miles an hour.

The winds stayed as light as this for the better part of two weeks. *Kylie* travelled fewer than sixty-nine miles, and managed to creep into and out of only five of the seventeen bays and inlets shown in Nigel's chartlets on the south coast of Roatan and Guanaja, the second-largest island of the group. During this time I was under way for only twenty-seven hours and twelve minutes, and 40% of the time was spent under engine. That any chartlets of Roatan were drawn, and that they blossomed with soundings and range-bearings, was due to Nigel's and Terrie's labours, not mine.

My day started at six-thirty, with a dive from the coachroof into water which was twenty-eight or twenty-nine degrees Celsius (82°-84°F) – far enough below body heat to give me a slight tingle but not nearly so cold as to shrink the flesh. Nevertheless, to me the water always looked far cooler than it really was, so I had to steel myself against the imagined cold. "Come on, this isn't the North Sea!" (Whose waters, even in summer, are colder than cellar beer.) "*Go now!*" I'd urge myself. "It'll only be a split second before you're in . . ." In spite of these urgings I would wangle a further moment's grace by pretending to balance on the balls of my feet before take-off and, when that had been done, I'd eke out another half-second to remind my ankles to stay together when they at last found themselves in mid-air.

Once I got underwater, though, it was difficult not to linger there. Below me, fronds of dark green eel-grass were being chivvied by a current, and above my left shoulder *Kylie*'s red hull was floating in a rose-pearl glow. Tiny blue-and-yellow fish glided out from a coral citadel, hung centre-stage, then suddenly wheeled about and darted off. Thirty feet ahead, the end-link of *Kylie*'s anchor chain raised itself from a bed of sand and sank back again as the warp slackened. I kicked upwards for air.

Re-boarding was done by placing a foot on the steering paddle of the wind-vane gear, a hand on one of a pair of oaken cheeks which clamped the gear to the rudder head, and the other hand on the stern capping. A moderate heave of the arms and a push of the foot was enough to get a knee on to the sternrail, and soon I was towelling my head.

After a panful of sugared porridge and half a pipe I would row across to *Nada*, where Terrie would be disentangling yesterday's washing from the guardrail while Nigel took down the awning and tumbled it through the forehatch. Pippin would be bent over her school books and her brother would be constructing Castillo de San Felipe from plastic blocks. Nigel would come into the cockpit gripping a ballpoint between his teeth, a much-folded chart in one hand and a pad of yellow foolscap in the other.

"Peter," he said, on one such morning in a voice considerably loud, "we must look into Fiddlers and Calabash bights, and the passage into Port Royal to the west of Lime Cays . . . and the shoal round Conch Cays needs checking out to see if there's room to anchor between the cays and the shore . . ."

"Right you are," I called as he strode forward to weigh *Nada*'s anchor. "I'll sail into whichever ones I can, and meet you again later."

Back in *Kylie*, I folded up the large awning and rigged a smaller one under the mainboom; then I shortened cable, hand-over-handing five fathoms of eight-plait nylon down the three-inch navel pipe into the cable locker. *Nada* gurgled past me under engine, Terrie at the tiller and Nigel high in the shrouds, taking back-bearings of a conspic. tree. I waited till *Kylie* had lurched in the quarter-wave before setting the mainsail. The wind might be a worthwhile five knots from the east but so as to get on with the day's work I swung the engine. Getting under way under sail would have been more satisfying, but it was nine o'clock already and those inlets had to be burrowed into . . .

Kylie puttered out of the overnight anchorage and headed south-eastward, wearing a genoa as soon as she had cleared the reef. Tentatively I put the engine into neutral. The bows bobbed uncertainly, as though trying to get into step with seas which were themselves in a pother because of having collided with other waves rebounding off the shore. A hundred yards seaward the rebounds petered out and *Kylie* settled into a nodding trot. Roatan and its unendearing insects fell astern and soon the rise and fall of the bow become so rhythmic and pleasing that I stoppped the engine and formed the view that surveying Roatan wasn't quite such a pressing matter as trimming *Kylie*'s sails . . .

What with one thing and another, by the time I crawled into the first inlet on the day's list *Nada* was disappearing behind a knobble of land farther eastward along the coast.

"Fiddlers Bight: Entry 320°, 150 yds wide between reefs. 25–40–35–30–20," I wrote, listing the soundings with only small satisfaction. I had nuzzled round the bight under engine, but had known while doing it that Nigel would already have written down much the same figures as I had.

I reached Port Royal in mid-afternoon, having sailed only nine miles against an adverse current and having gone into only Fiddlers Bight. I dinghied across to *Nada*, carrying in my shirt pocket a mere half-page of findings; and, soon afterwards, rowed back to *Kylie* snorting smoke. *Nada* had covered twice the distance and Nigel's foolscap had been thick with figures.

After a week of such meagre results I was getting through an ounce of tobacco a day, much surveying of bights and cays still needed to be done and time was running short. We decided to split tacks, hoping that between us we might cover more ground. On the tenth day *Nada* left Old Port Royal to survey Trujillo Bay, thirty-five miles distant on mainland Honduras, while *Kylie* headed for the Guanaja Settlement, twelve miles nearer. We left Old Port Royal in a twelve-knot easterly, but as *Kylie* beat away from the land, in the course of an hour it veered thirty degrees and fell to five knots. My hopes of making a passage under sail fell with it. On and off, the engine was running for six hours that day, for although the wind strengthened to fifteen knots for a few minutes during the afternoon the current increased too, and with it the height and length of the waves. With her laden waterline length of twenty-one feet, *Kylie* hobby-horsed among them, making between three and four knots under mainsail and engine but – owing to the current and the angle of wind – only two or three over the ground.

Minutes after sunset, still seven miles short of The Settlement, I made out the white triangle of *Nada*'s foresail pitching eastward against the green background of the island. The morning's wind-veer and stronger current had converted her original cross-wind course for Trujillo into a header, so she too had stood back inshore and was making for The Settlement.

In glistening moonlight *Kylie* stole past two miles of invisible reefs and anchored in five fathoms in the lee of the town. As on Up and Down, the wooden houses of The Settlement were huddled on a small cay to seaward of the main island and open to the wind which, here, set electric bulbs swinging above striped tablecloths. Here, people were lifting glasses, bending over plates, leaning back in chairs and slapping shoulders. I stood the kerosene lantern in the cockpit and shaved off two days' stubble, for there were no mosquitoes and the air carried odours of crushed shrimps from the fishing boats which jostled against the wooden piles, diesel-spills at the fuel dock, musky clapboard, ripe bananas, rice-grains bubbling in pots, and chickens roasting over fires of husk.

"Beautify Guanaja!" said notices pinned to posts and pasted onto the clapboard when I rowed ashore into the hurly-burly. Built on taller stilts than those at Up and Down, the houses were painted less brightly but the boardwalks were bustling. You had to watch your step, though, for some stilts were rickety. After twice putting my foot on to thin air I hobbled into a place where I ordered pork cutlets and drank white rum.

"You off of a sailboat?"

Long dark face, deep creases from nostrils to jaw, and between them a slit of a mouth.

"Yes; and you . . .?"

"Mine's a hell-hole an' its owner is an asshole. He fucked the motor coming down from Isla Mujeres. We were supposed to be going to Cartagena in a hurry. Like, he needed to get to Cartagena yesterday. You going to Cartagena?"

"Sorry, no."

"You never said about going to Cartagena," said a fluffy-haired woman with light brown legs who kept a hand across his knee; "till now, you never did say it."

"What you telling me? I'm always talkin' 'bout Cartagena. Cartagena is a beautiful city . . .!"

" . . . and Guanaja is a beautiful island."

"Guanaja is a heap of steaming hogshit. Just you look at that sticker: 'Beautify Guanaja,' it says."

"But I really like it out here," said the woman, squeezing his knee; "there aren't no mosquitoes, an' we can lay out on deck under the stars . . ."

8

Tommy Atkins in Sepia

The sun slapped me awake. I sniffed. Overnight, the Settlement's pleasing odours had turned into stenches. Aboard *Nada* Nigel unfolded a chart and fingered his beard. Before getting back to Guatemala by no later than the end of the month he needed to survey the north coast of Guanaja and the mainland coast from Trujillo Bay westward to Tela, taking in the offlying Cayos Cochinos as he went. It looked to be about one hundred and fifty miles as the crow flew; in the previous week he had surveyed only thirty-five. If the winds stayed as light as they were at present he would run out of time before the task was half done.

We weighed up the ifs and buts of splitting tacks again, Nigel humming quite a lot and me harring a little. In order of priority, the north coast of Guanaja came first and Trujillo last.

"Let me have a go at Cabo de Honduras and Trujillo by myself," I said, "so as to give you more time to cover the important bits."

Cabo de Honduras is the blade of the sickle of land which forms Trujillo Bay, Punto Caxinas is the point of the sickle and Trujillo town is on the handle. Punto Caxinas lies twenty-five miles south-by-west of The Settlement, across the prevailing wind and current. The wind might be light but I wanted to make the crossing under sail.

I weighed at nine-thirty, in an easterly of no more than six knots. Within the hour it had inched higher and *Kylie* was in five hundred fathoms, logging five knots. I set the wind-vane and left her to head southwards while I expanded the chart.

Drawn to a scale of about $4^1/_4$ miles to the inch, the chart was adequate for the crossing to the mainland but was on too small a scale to record the many soundings I was hoping to harvest in Trujillo Bay. I enlarged it three-fold on squared paper and fought off feelings of triumph. In less than one hour, Trujillo Bay had grown by $3^1/_2$ inches.

By two in the afternoon *Kylie* had logged nineteen miles and the light-tower on Punto Caxinas had risen above a low forest of mangroves. Close to the point the water became suddenly thick and green, separated from the current by a ribbon of froth. I steered downwind of the froth until the light-tower was past the beam, then pointed upwind on the port tack, with the castle of Trujillo far off on the leeward bow.

Onshore to windward lay a wrecked ship. I stared at it.

Though many ship-remains are lying above water on the coasts of the world, the sea does not often keep them looking like ships for very long. A vessel runs aground, and a couple of years later all that is left is a rusty skeleton on a foreshore. A long-standing, identifiable, above-water shipwreck is quite rare. Looking back over fifteen years of cruising *Kylie*, I could remember seeing only three: a broken-backed oil tanker in the Dardanelles; a funnel, masts and superstructure in Bantry Bay; and a 4000-ton trader on Lighthouse Reef, off Belize. None of these ships could have been more than twenty years old, and its wrecking no more than five. By now their above-water parts will have been depleted to rusty stumps. I had seen these ships, had wondered about their strandings, and had gone on my way.

But I could not pass this one by, for it seemed to me that I had seen it before.

She was six thousand tons gross, with a dead-straight stem and a curved counter stern, a tall smokestack topped by a narrow-rimmed cowl, an amidships superstructure, a small wheelhouse forward of the funnel and an emergency wheel on the poop. Below decks lay coal-fired boilers which, fed with best Welsh coal, had themselves fed steam into a triple-expansion reciprocating engine which had delivered 600 horsepower to a propeller shaft; riveted plating with butt straps; keel laid seventy years ago in, probably, Antwerp. She was still upright but her stern was higher out of the water than it should have been even when in ballast, and her bows were half underwater. Hull holed, but not broken-backed; much rusted, but still some black paint on the funnel and white on the wheelhouse. A wreck, but still a recognizable ship.

I sailed towards her and anchored near. The reverse curve of her counter stern was haunting. The old *Empire Test* had had the same line, counter-curving gently forward before plunging narrowly downward like . . .? Like . . ..? Like – to snapshot it in sepia – the heel of a Ginger Rogers shoe.

Launched in 1923 as *Thysville* to ply to the Belgian Congo, after the Second World War she had been re-named *Empire Test* and given the task of transporting troops between Britain and the Empire. Though her flag was British her livery had a distinctive Anglo-Saxon bias, the hull being cricket-flannel white, girdled by a band of Saxe blue.

In 1950 the body of the Empire was still breathing. It had lost some major organs but its heart was ticking and its spirit was quite lively, with ninety-nine Archbishops and Right Reverend Bishops ministering to the Anglican congregations in Africa alone. Other verities, too, were holding up: India was still to be seen now and then at Lord's. On the other hand, some unsporting types on the darkest continent were not playing the game at all. White planters had been hacked to death in Kenya, so a battalion of troops was being sent out to remind the natives of what the rules were.

Cargo liner, *circa* 1923.

Empire Test had set off on her imperial duty in style, played away down the Mersey by a regimental band, steaming out to sea from a Liverpool in which maroon-and-cream tramcars with wooden seats still clanged past a statue of Queen Victoria, fifty years dead but by no means forgotten. The statue had weathered into various shades of green, and so too had some of the sentiments which went with it. We knew that we were in a troopship which was transporting Guardsmen in 1950 battledress to Mombasa but – what with the coal dust, the counter stern, and black gang shovelling down below, we felt that we were shipping Tommy Atkins to somewhere east of Suez, where there weren't no Ten Commandments an' a man could raise a thirst; that we were leaving England, home and beauty to give the fuzzy-wuzzies a thorough drubbing . . .

So as to put Atkins in to bat before the Eternal Umpire drew stumps, *Empire Test* went flat out, doing sometimes as much as fourteen knots. While this speed did not put her among the ocean greyhounds, she was not by any means a snail. The average speed of the average cargo ship in 1950 was about eleven miles an hour, so fourteen knots was considered good going. For two hours in the middle of the watch, when the boiler fires had been raked and she had built up a head of steam, *Empire Test*'s forefoot would scamper through the seas. She couldn't keep up the fast pace for long, though; towards the end of the watch her speed might fall to as low as eight knots if the coal was poor and the firebars had become clogged with clinker. What she had an abundance of, whatever speed she went at, was an aura of Empire, fading but still heady.

Now, gazing at the wreck in Trujillo Bay, it was difficult not to feel a sense of loss. Once upon a time, Tommy Atkins had held sway in the Bay Islands and on this Mosquito Coast too . . .

"What's that that hirples at my side?"
The foe that you must fight, my lord.
"That rides as fast as I can ride?"
The shadow of your might, my lord.

9
Trujillo Bay

Overtaking me was an unpoetical blur which in minutes had hardened into a jungle-green assault craft hung about with motor-tyres and bristling with soldiers, the nearest of whom were carrying rifles. They caught up with *Kylie* in the middle of the bay, between the wreck and Trujillo town. Eyeing the tyres, I hung my largest fenders from the guardrail.

"You must go back this minute to the *comandancia*," declared a *mestizo* sergeant with reptilian eyes and a wispy moustache.

"Eh . . .? But, see here, I have a cruising permit for Trujillo . . ."

"That's no good," he said, prodding at the document obtained at great expense in Coxen's Hole. "This is a military area. ENTRY PROHIBITED. You must come now to the *comandancia*."

I dug into a locker.

"Cigarette?" I said, fiddling with the cellophane wrapper.

"Do let me help you," said the soldier.

"Oh, I *see* . . . You'd like the *whole* pack . . .? Well now, sergeant, the wind is *no mucho* and believe you me my engine isn't very *mucho* either. Perhaps it might be possible for the wind to get me to Trujillo this morning, and perhaps this afternoon, when the wind is stronger, I could get to your *comandancia* . . .?"

"Very well, then; I permit you to report to the *comandancia* this afternoon," he said, tapping a cigarette on his thumbnail before passing the packet to his comrades. "The port captain must issue you with another *zarpe*, and . . . er . . . have you a match . . .? Or possibly, a lighter . . .?"

I anchored in two fathoms off Trujillo, near the Bar Cintra Negra, where a stout Black Carib in a finely woven straw hat tied two donkeys to palings and afterwards poured me coffee from an enamelled, two-decker jug. Though forefathered by British-owned slaves who had been captured by the Spanish while in transit in chains to Roatan, he said he didn't have it in him to grind axes. He smiled broadly as he said this, his teeth gleamimg brighter than the jug. Mind me, he went on, Lieutenant Barnsley and those of my countrymen who came after him had bombarded Trujillo quite heavily so as to get even with the Spaniards, taking off, in the process, his great-great-grandaddy's head. But *entonces*, *mi amigo*, all that was ancient hist'ry . . .. Whichever way the world had tilted in centuries past it did not upset his level-headed, up-to-date view of his fellow men: a whip was everywhere a whip, whoever's hand held it. These days, him and me were in the same boat, didn't I think . . .? Here we were in Trujillo, not a hundred years after the *latígo* was declared illegal, both of us being lashed into line again by the CIA and the KGB. But, he said while putting aside the coffee jug and pouring me out a beer, we must see the situation in the round like I was so clearly intent on doing. Why not contemplate it, therefore, like the gentleman of leisure that I was, from the back of one of his fine donkeys? On them, we could get to the castle in comfort and view – albeit from afar – the wreck I was asking him about. Uh . . .? Come again . . .? Well, it had been lying there longer than he could remember . . . because, uh, the seas in that corner of the bay were never ever big. Hurricanes hardly happened in Honduras, he said in effect when I was taking my leave of him after a third beer, and Nigel Calder ought to mention the fact in his guidebook . . .

Sounding as I went, I coasted past two miles of dowdy jungle which had no conspic. anythings in it and anchored near where the sickle-shaped blade on my chart was separated from its handle by a narrow creek. Beyond two sandy fingers at the mouth of the creek lay a five-mile lagoon which was surrounded by dense mangroves. The lagoon would be alive with mosquitoes but in Barnsley's day it had been a passable haven, with a depth of five feet at its entrance.

The water offshore was cloudy, so I rowed towards the entrance, poling as I went, and carried a good seven feet until the fingers of sand were at their closest, when the seabed suddenly shelved to three and a half. I poled the thick dark water between the fingers of sand but nowhere found greater depths. The shallow bar was only ten yards wide; once over it I found water ten feet deep but *Kylie* could not possibly cross the bar and reach it. I wrote "$3^1/_2$ft" in black ballpoint on my chart, pulled a face at the image of St Christopher screwed to the starboard side of the companionway, and made sail for the port captain's office.

Right from the start he was at pains to be a more helpful port captain than the tyrant at Coxen's Hole. Smiling, affable, worldly-wise but not jaded, eager to put me at my ease: every little thing about him was in close harmony with some other little thing. His khaki trousers were held up by a tan-coloured belt, fastened with a solid buckle which shone warmly. His demerara shoes toned with his trousers and their toecaps travelled neatly across the same number of tiles at each step. The two notepads on his shining desktop were as equidistant from the packet of cigarettes lying at its centre as each of his bright quick eyes was from his shining, dead-straight nose. All things considered, I felt inclined to spit.

"You know Texas? I have a cousin in Dallas."

"Er . . . sorry; I'm from Great Britain."

"How *stupid* of me!" He made a fist and punched his own midriff. "Mrs Thatcher is a wonderful woman, eh?"

He charged twenty-three lempiras, including the *mordida*.

I walked a dusty path from the office to the foreshore, by-passing a two-storey roofless ruin, once a hospital, near which half a dozen soldiers were punting a football. On the foreshore three officers were eating lunch at a table outside a white tent. It was impossible to avoid them.

"Good afternoon," I said, walking on towards *Kylie*'s dinghy on the beach. Before I could reach it a sentry stepped out from behind a tumbledown wall and, by jerking his rifle and clicking his tongue, signalled I must go back to the officers. His eyes were granite pebbles.

Outside the tent a hand lifted a fork and jabbed it towards *Kylie*.

"Move that boat this minute or I will use it for target practice."

I sailed two miles to the head of the bay and re-anchored in ten feet. A black boy tied his *cayuco* astern and wriggled up into the cockpit, where he watched me renew a frayed whipping.

"What is your age?"

"Eleven."

Eleven . . .? His skull was man-sized but his legs were as thin as kindling sticks. Honduras, said the guidebook again, was the poorest of all the Central American republics; and the people in this black boy's township, it seemed, were a rung or two further down the ladder than the white people at Up and Down were.

I tipped a bag of lines onto the duckboard under the boy's feet. He picked out a length of braided polyester.

"*Cuerda*," he said.

"Rope," I told him. "For you . . . *Por tú*."

While he practised making bowlines I cooked us a couple of

omelettes, filling them with grated cheese; but when he had left, paddling his little *cayuco* towards a light winking at us from the trees, I hoisted the dinghy aboard my boat and lashed it down firmly to the coachroof.

10
Cochino Grande

At dawn the sky was one-eighth fluffy cloud and the deck glistened with dew. I weighed at a quarter to seven and poled out both genoas for the run to Los Cayos Cochinos, thirty miles downwind. *Kylie* glided past the *comandancia*, the tent, the tumbledown wall and its impassive sentry, the roofless hospital, the shipwreck, and the light-tower on Punto Caxinas. I latched-in the wind-vane, streamed the log and waited for the wind to build.

By noon the log read twenty-one miles, yet for the first four hours the wind had seemed no stronger than eight or ten knots, just enough to set the Red Ensign lurching between the backstays but not nearly enough to stream it truly. The backs of the waves were dinted only lightly, like damp sand is if pressed by a spoon, yet *Kylie* had been making four knots. Now, at noon, some wave-tops were purling briefly down their faces and I was logging more than five miles in the hour. I stood on the coachroof, splay-footed against the rolling, braced between the shrouds and the mast. To the south-east a 4000-foot peak on the mainland still showed through the haze. I dropped the shades on the sextant into place and pulled down the sun, turning the tangent-screw till the sun's lower lip was kissing the horizon, then I swung the sextant on the axis of its telescope, made a last adjustment to the screw and, by-and-by, said "Hup!" to myself. Five minutes later, having worked out the noon latitude, I drew a half-inch pencil line on US chart 28150 (Tela to Barratasca) and crossed it with a bearing of the mainland peak. According to bearings, *Kylie* was ten and a half miles from the easternmost point of Los Cayos Cochinos. I stowed away the sextant in its box, clambered back into the cockpit and stared ahead.

The waves were a little larger, their backs scalloped more clearly by the wind, and the runnels were happening more often and lasting longer. Now *Kylie* was rolling ten or fifteen degrees each way and the wind-vane was swinging through forty degrees between the rolls, yanking the tiller after it as it went. I tightened the shockcords but the tiller did not stop its antics. "Grr-grrah! Grr-grrah!" snarled the tiller at the wind-vane, lunging from side to side like a dog with its lead between its teeth.

I straddled the cockpit, hands gripping the lip of the keyhole- shaped companionway as the booms dipped and rose, shearing the sky and sea. Between *Kylie* and the seemingly far – but in reality only 2.8 miles away – horizon, the sea-colours ahead changed from sparkling opal to ultramarine, finishing in a hard sharp line of Prussian blue.

After a while there appeared a faint grey hump above the Prussian blue.

"Hrr-a-a-hh!" shrieked the tiller to the wind-vane.

"For Heaven's sake . . .!" I chided, casting off the shock-cords and grabbing the tiller. Making a landfall was an allowable reason for a small outcry but it was not a happening about which to go berserk. When it's weeks since you last saw land and days since you glimpsed the sun or stars, and when you've been going entirely by dead reckoning, making a landfall gives a blip of pleasure, it's true. Your arithmetic has worked out so that your boat has carried you to within eyeshot of where you calculated it would, so a good-oh! might be in order. But here and now, only three hours since you lost sight of a light-tower, with the weather fair and the bilge dry, why remark on it at all? You haven't won the lottery, laddie; it's just a local landfall.

But I murmured an extra word or two when *Kylie* sailed closer to this latest landfall, the Lion's Head of Cochino Grande, the easternmost of the Los Cayos Cochinos, the Hog Islands. By this time the wind was Force 5, and six-foot swells were breaking on the reefs, making seething, bilious seas, above which the Lion's Head rose five hundred feet. Eyeless, fanged, shaking its mane of trees and growling fretfully at every wetting of its chin, it looked a surly beast.

Kylie came up to the headland warily, leaning well away from its bony shoulder. As she rounded it I glimpsed a scatter of lesser islands. They looked interesting, but a close inspection would have to wait, for the lion's mane was tossing and a fierce gust had swept down, heeling *Kylie* over till the sidedeck was awash. I downed helm and luffed up. Before me opened the bay of Cochino Grande.

The high land above the bay was bold but not rough. Its steep flanks were covered densely by trees so that any severities were stippled and softened by foliage. From the high bluff of the Lion's Head a mile-long spine sloped down to the sea, curving beneath the trees into small beaches separated from each other by rocky outcrops to form natural cubicles with differently textured walls and floors. Here, a twenty-yard beach was bounded on one side by a smooth grey buttress and on the other by pocked boulders. There, a fifty-yard cove was carpeted by grass rather than sand and was screened from its neighbour by jagged rocks on which stood white pelicans. To one side of the pelicans a palomino horse was rolling in a small meadow. I wanted to go ashore and join it.

First, though, I had to find the boar that lurked in the middle of the bay.

I had put away US 28150 and was using a chart made from a Honduran government survey. It was a land-map rather than a sea-chart; the local equivalent to a British Ordnance Survey but with stronger colours, and with contours drawn at twenty-metre intervals. Ramblers would love that map. At a glance they could know how steep were the gullies or how high above sea-level were the eyebrows of the Lion's Head across which they had scrambled. From it, they could work out how many metres they were elevated above the deck of the small yacht which appeared to be loitering in the middle of the bay, or – if they happened to be looking at it closely through binoculars – above the lone occupant presently scratching his head in its cockpit.

Not very helpfully for that occupant, no sea-depths had been shown on the chart. As if to make up for this, the mapmaker had drawn the underwater features with a degree of emphasis which verged on the lurid. To tell the truth, he had rather overdone it. His map of the sea-bed was a nightmare of burrs, spikes, pricks and barbs. Porcupined reefs quivered against tumescent headlands, coral clumps were shown as spiked maces and the channels between the islands appeared to be infested with a species of gigantic cacti. And all was done in such sharp clear detail that the dangers looked as though they were not several feet under the water but merely inches under your very nose. It was difficult not to feel that if you put a finger on the map it would come away running blood.

By far the most fearsome danger shown on the chart was a bristly boar-shaped reef standing four-square in the middle of the bay. It looked monstrous, this boar. With beetling shoulders, sharp tusks, spiked tail and bristles, he was the lord of the Hog Islands. I didn't want *Kylie* getting within touching distance of any single one of the horrors shown on the map, but particularly not the boar. If *Kylie* got herself between those tusks she'd be a goner.

I stood on the coachroof and scanned the water ahead. There was no

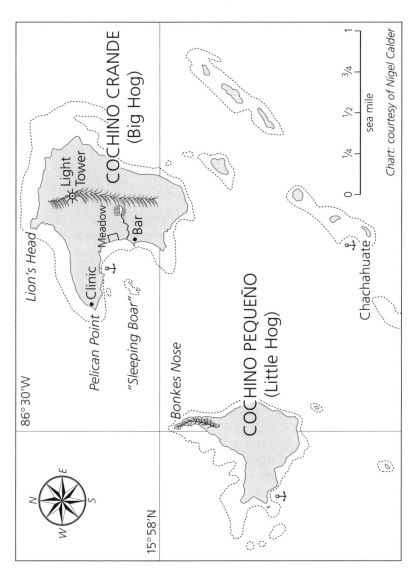

Chart 5: Los Cayos Cochinos or Hog Islands.

sign of the boar – but the sun was somewhat in my eyes. Thinking that the sun's angle and the ruffled surface of the bay might be deceiving me, I climbed to the spreaders and looked again.

After two long looks I returned to the cockpit, gripped the tiller and headed straight for where the boar was; and a minute later I ran over it where it lay deeply asleep, eight feet below the keel.

Later still, bringing his beer glass with him, an American visitor to the island got up from a deeply cushioned chair and frowned at the divers' map on the wall. The map was four times the size of mine, and on it the reef looked more distinctly like a boar, I insisted, than any other creature on God's earth.

He put the glass to his lips and drank.

"W-e-l-l-l," he came out eventually, "I believe that it looks more like a South American armadillo. I *know* that because I've shot 'um."

We contemplated local relics on display in a showcase below the map. On the lowest shelf lay pot-shards, the largest of which was rhomboid, with a slightly bowed outer surface no more than an inch and a half across. We agreed that it was a fragment of an ancient jar, but was it Arawak, Carib, Maya, or Paya?

"Hard to know, sirs," said their finder from behind the bar.

"Ever try carbon-dating 'um?" said the American.

The grey building which housed the bar slid behind a grey rock as my dinghy slid onto the white beach at the edge of the meadow, where the palomino watched me from a distance and two golden labradors loped up to snuffle my corduroyed knees.

"You'll see a path," said a man, pointing his machete uphill at trees.

With the labradors scouting ahead, I set off to climb to the island's light-tower, out of sight behind trees on the peak. At first the path was easy to keep to, but soon I lost it among a tumble of rocks, from which I was retrieved by the dogs. Nosing the gritty, stony hillside they took turns at shepherding me upwards, one wagging encouragement as I floundered through leafy scree, while his companion roared into the forest to demolish sundry obstacles – cardboard boxes, by the sound of them – which the cartographer had overlooked.

Panting, we at last got to what I supposed was the top. The map said we were now 143 metres above the Caribbean, so the theoretical horizon should be twenty-five miles away, but I could see nothing of it. On all sides and above, branches and leaves shut us off from the sea – and from Heaven too, for the canopy was pierced only scantly by sunbeams. It was one o'clock on a tropical afternoon but the light was the same as on an October day in England. I watched for leaf-falls; the dogs sat on their haunches.

"Why not find it for me?" I suggested while smoking half a pipe, but they rushed off downhill, woofing. I made along the spine alone, forcing my way through a thicket of branches and lianas till I came upon the Big Hog light. It was mounted on an open-work tower of bolted angle-bars which rose from slivers of ashen bark. I brushed away the bark-fall with my fingers, hoping to find a memento to go with those from Up and Down; but the lettering on the manufacturer's nameplate when I found it said "Made in Germany".

I picked my way slowly downhill till I became entangled in a fall of trees which lay canted and skewed, trunk over limb, pungent with decay. Inching sideways across a leprous branch above a canyon which was looking more like death's dark vale with every passing second, I fell. Troglodytes stuffed maggots up my nostrils and pelted me with wormwood before dropping me, with a loud cackle, into a vat of ink.

My tobacco kept dry, though. This miracle was discovered by my fingers minutes later when they tugged a soggy pouch from my left-hand trouser pocket and fumbled tobacco flakes into the pipe bowl. Puffing St Bruno, limping a bit, wading through knee-deep ink onto a bank of damp sand, I wished that the fragments of the day might drop into a recognisable pattern before its end. Perhaps the port captain's aims in life at Trujillo had not been so ridiculous after all. Weren't harmonious matchings what everyone tried for? Life was thought to run more sweetly as a result. We meshed cogs with wheels and Jacks with Jills; matched tops to bottoms, sail-plans to hulls; and so – whatever the American had said – Cochino Grande had to have a Big Boar in its bay . . . though its light, which I had expected to have been made by Chance Brothers in Birmingham, had been oddly foreign. So far, there'd been one neat match and one mis-match in the day. Two down and one to go; there was still the pot-shard to be matched up with an urn before the day could end satisfactorily . . .. At the end of this dark vale I'd surely find a clue to the provenance of those shards. Perhaps round the next corner a Mayan with a bun-shaped hair-do would be silhouetted against a bright white beach and a beryl-blue bay, kneading maize dough in a chipped brown bowl . . .

The gully gave onto a sandy cove a hundred paces south of the palomino's meadow but, like the other coves, when I got there it was empty.

I waded through crystal shallows above slabs of dun-coloured rock on which sea anemones rolled in the surge, waved on by polyps. Towards Pelican Point the water deepened, so I rowed the dinghy round the point and came to a stone-walled house and, alongside it, a small clinic. It was in a lush and beautiful setting, backed by the peak above the Lion's Head, in green shade freshened by breezes which eddied from the peak down to a lively sea. Under a salmon-pink orchid outside the clinic sat a Black Carib woman holding a numbered tag. Her face was blotched grey from jawbone to temple and her right eye was seeping mucus. I learned that she had been carried a hundred miles through mountains and swamps on a litter before being ferried acoss from the mainland by boat. Here at the clinic she would be treated by an American nurse who gave her services without charge and dispensed medicines whose shelf-life in the USA had expired.

The woman watched me walk into the sea, rinse my diving-mask and fit the snorkel. I swam the reef for an hour, hoping to see a great amount of brain coral, tunicate coral, angel fish and wrasse, but much of the coral had died and there were few fish. From the bench outside the clinic the woman with the suppurating eye stared at me again when I lay down in the shade.

By then, the wind from the Lion's Head was blowing differently, and above the woman's head the orchid was leaping like a candle flame does before it goes out.

11
Chachahuate

I sailed to a lean piglet of an island lying in the surf a mile or so south of the Big Hog. The island was the size of Up, and fifty people were living on it in a hamlet of grass huts, *palapas*, which on some maps is labelled Chachahuate.

Kylie came to the island from the north-east, anchoring in a patch of turquoise water among coral-clusters the colour of saffron and cinammon. The boat lay quietly, shielded by the furlong of sand from the trade wind swell and from the surf spuming on the reef. Above me flew pelicans and frigate birds, and on the sand to windward the *palapas* stood among palms, their thatch dappled by sunbeams and the threshing shadows of palm leaves. It was a modern travel-brochure idyll, but Pinzón, de Solis and Coxen would have recognized it, and Owen and Barnsley would have known it as well, complete with the *cayucos* at the water's edge, covered then as now with palm leaves against the sun's rays.

I set about covering my own boat against them.

While I was spreading the awning a Black Carib paddled out in a *cayuco*, dipping the blade to the left and giving the shaft a flickery twist before bringing it up for the next stroke. Its charred sides blackened further by rains, leaking through a gash in the bow, the *cayuco* had been hollowed-out by fire and its owner looked as if he, too, had been through an inferno. His arms and eyebrows were singed white and his face had the look and texture of scorched leather.

"Is it safe here?" I called, thinking about the anchor-holding and the nearby coral heads.

"Sir, nobodys will thief you! And it is I, Michael, who tells you!"

"Would you like a coffee, Michael?"

The leather split wide open, exposing gapped teeth. "Later, man, later! I got to get me to de clinic 'cos me head is killin' me, God diggit!"

I rowed to the beach. White sand burned my feet. Children ran to me, jabbing fingers at the dinghy.

"Come back! You must not molest him. He is a guest."

The speaker brushed sand grains off a bench and poured me a beer. He was a *Garifuna*, a Black Carib, and, like his fellow countryman at Trujillo, was wearing a fine straw hat.

With sails cobbled from plastic sacks but which looked as delicately beautiful as a butterfly's wings, a *cayuco* scudded towards us. Soon afterwards a small boy trudged up the beach carrying a red snapper.

"Tomàs, I bring your dinner."

"Chachahuate," said Tomàs, palms upwards in the shade of his hat, "is Paradise. I have a big house in La Ceiba but I am here at Chachahuate, living in a little hut. Why . . .? Because La Ceiba has too many people . . .!"

He inspected my glass again and wiped its rim a second time. "The c'rect population for Paradise is fifty! More than fifty persons, an' nobody knows nobody . . .. You take my meaning . . .m'm? You got a family . . . m'm?"

"Yes."

"Here," he said proudly, "we are all family . . .! Truly, it is Paradise."

The scene could have been Biblical. To the right, a brother-in-law was mending nets, plying a wooden shuttle in the shade. Gathered about him, nephews talked of the fish they hoped to catch, their eyes moving from the nets to the sea and back again, knotting the one to the other. A second *cayuco* dropped its sail and glided silently into the shallows. People clustered around it and began to clean the morning's catch, working silently, without fuss. There was no harsh noise except the rasp of surf on the distant reef, no hurried movement except the sudden plummet of a pelican or the swoop of a frigate bird. Tomàs carried a gleaming fish into his hut and came out beaming.

"A fine one, eh?"

Yes, I said, his main course was going to be excellent, but where was he getting water to drink it down with, I wondered, and fruit for his afters? After all, didn't Eden have an apple tree . . .?

Water was no problem for Chachahuate, he said: Cousin Michael would be back from Cochino Grande with five gallons within the hour, and some quite lovely fruit would be coming in from La Ceiba . . ."

"In *cayucos*?"

"Maybe in motorboat; maybe in *cayuco* . . ."

He was stretching things a bit. La Ceiba lay sixteen miles away and the sea would be rucked into five-foot waves if the trades blew just a little stronger. In which case, Cousin Michael couldn't possibly get here from La Ceiba in his leaky log . . .. I drank my beer and stood up.

"Work to do," I said briskly. Tomàs shook his head. What work would that be, he wondered?

I told him about Nigel's guidebook and about what the army officer had threatened to do at Trujillo. Tomàs tilted his hat and smacked his lips.

"You see . . ..! Don't I tell you true? If more than fifty live in a place it cannot be a paradise."

I stayed at Chachahuate for another day and a star-filled night, during which time I noted in the logbook that the first pelicans were airborne at 4.52 a.m. and that people were up and about before the birds, bobbing lanterns along the beach at 4.35, lighting fires and casting for bait-fish.

But not all people in Paradise were early risers. At ten-thirty in the morning Michael still lay sprawled beneath a palm tree, moaning. Missie Jan's drugs had damped down the raging fire in his head, God diggit, but only Cousin Tomàs could dispense lubricant for his neck. By eleven-thirty Michael was high on rum but low on cash, and, close cousin or not, Tom's was refusing to pour him any more neck oil. The refusal brought a hurricane of oaths that toppled Tomàs off his chair. He picked himself up and brandished a paddle. Michael lunged at him, roaring . . .

When the rumpus had died down I sailed towards a cluster of reefs to the far south-west of Chachahuate, searching for Providence Shoal – "Rep (1907) PD", according to the chart. Soon a twelve-knot wind was raising three-foot seas and the satnav was stating that the tail of the shoal was lying a further mile south-west of the PD on the chart. *Kylie* lay hove-to off its tail, helm a-lee, head seventy degrees to the wind, while I inked-in the amendment, put a kettle on the stove and worked out how the shoal had got its name.

In 1629 the Earl of Warwick had founded the Providence Company to colonize islands off the Mosquito Coast, and by 1635 had established a trading station on Roatan, 370 miles to the north-west. It was not difficult to suppose, waiting for a kettle to boil, that two cables to windward of *Kylie*, full fathom five on my extension of Providence Shoal, lay the remains of the Company's flagship. Three hundred tons burthen, coming to the Bay Islands from the west, standing out from the unfriendly Spanish mainland towards Old Port Royal on Roatan, lying six points to a fickle early-morning trade wind and making only a knot through the water, glimpsing from the foretop the palms of Chachahuate safely to weather before being carried onto those eight-foot-deep coral patches by the current . . .

"Hoy!"

It wasn't a hail from a shipwrecked mariner but a cry from me. I'd taken my tea into the cockpit, and there, fifty yards distant, was a naked Black Carib paddling a hollowed-out log ten feet long and two and a half feet in beam, fifteen-inch freeboard at the bow and a hand-span at

Toiling to another Eden.

the stern, making two knots or more into lumpy seas, with a stem of green bananas at his feet. Twelve miles of sea behind him but four still to go, digging forward with his paddle forty-two times a minute, shoulders aching, knees smarting, face and body running water: the sight made my toes curl.

But as I watched him labouring onwards through the waves it seemed that his body was not running water but was glistening jewels; that he was not a nameless black man carrying a stem of green bananas from the mainland to an offshore sandbank, but was Adam toiling eastwards to another Eden.

Again I lifted my hand and waved it, not expecting any return except a flash of white teeth. But, marvellously, he interrupted the plunging rhythm of his stroke to raise an arm and wave back.

And when I thought how that naked man had been shut out from prosperity by circumstance of birth, his mother carried on a litter through stinking swamps to be anointed with the discarded medicaments of the rich, himself transported in chains, whipped, *mordida* upon *mordida*, sucked by mosquitoes; how his suffering had been allowed so that I might eat cheap bananas and blue-eyed men in boardrooms might spend their weekends playing polo with a prince or sucking his royal sister-in-law's toes; and when I went on to think how far that black man in the most primitive of boats was outdistancing them and me on his voyage towards a second Paradise, it seemed to me that he was the richer. It was not only the breaking waves that were vesting him in jewels, it was the way he was journeying through them.

I drained my mug and rinsed it. Tomàs had spoken truly about the miles that could be covered by a lone man in a *cayuco* but was he right about Chachahuate? Was the picture-postcard island on the horizon even a demi-paradise? True, there were no mosquitoes at Chachahuate, but there had been no mosquitoes on Up and Down, either. And at Chachahuate there had been the rum and the upraised paddle, and the weeping eye in the grey face outside the clinic . . .

I hardened the sheets, turned *Kylie* towards the wind and set a course for the meeting-place with *Nada*.

12

Dolours and Scents

". . . a woman will endure a long journey nearly as well as a man, and certainly better than a horse or bullock. They are invaluable in picking up and retailing information and hearsay gossip, which will give clues to much of importance, that, unassisted, you might miss."

SIR FRANCIS GALTON *The Art of Travel* (1855)

It was that delicate moment between night and morning when the heroine tucks another six inches of nightgown between her knees and the hero at last stops grinding his teeth. At sea on the same meridian the light on Cabo Tres Puntas had gone out but I did not take note of it, for writing had become almost as much of a problem as making love. The pencil was worn down to a stub and my ballpoint had run dry. I peeled the wrapper from the last choc-bar and poured methylated spirit into the Primus bowl. Watching the blue flame lick at the burner, I asked myself if there really was a need to record that *Kylie* was wearing a 92 sq-ft foresail as she entered Amatique Bay; that I had handed the mainsail so as not to arrive at the Rio Dulce before 0545, the time of sunrise; and that the low swells coming from astern would soon break on the reefs to the north, releasing energy at a rate incalculable in old-fashioned foot-pounds by me or even, perhaps, in up-to-date Newtons by Nigel.

Before the kettle boiled I had given up writing pilotage notes about the Northwest Caribbean. Nigel's survey had come to an end and in a few short hours I would be at Mario's watching a video.

I bit into the choc-bar. The oil lamp shone on the boomerang from which *Kylie* had taken her name; shone on a painting of Majorcan orange-trees, and on another of the castle above Keköva Roads where a young Turk had saved two women from slavery; and lastly – as a glint of England, home and beauty – shone on an enamelled picture of the Suffolk coast. I had travelled thousands of miles since leaving it, but whether they would be accounted miles made good was quite another matter . . .

In the margin of the chart my wobbling pencil drew a series of rickety five-barred gates which added up, after a while, to 14 years 4 months and 6 days. I sucked fudge from under my tongue . . .

Dear, I have been covering the miles tolerably well, and I'm sure you would enjoy being here, for there are wonderful sights to be seen and good times to be had, Kylie *stays snug and dry, so that even in heavy weather you could smoke, though they'd not be Player's Navy Cut at four-and-tenpence for twenty.*

This last month has seen me among islands which our atlas says aren't there. On two the people speak only English; and on another they call their place Paradise. Seeing the ailments that afflict them, you'll say they ought to call it Paracetamol . . .

Slowly the wind dropped away and the daylight grew dimmer. There came a low rumble of thunder from the west, followed soon after by heavy rain. It was as if Lago Izabal were being forced through a huge colander only inches above the masthead. The velvety dawn seascape with a lighthouse to the south and Venus gleaming in the east became a roaring cistern. The small seas that had been dancing alongside in company were instantly hammered flat, and, as the deluge increased, the surface of the bay erupted, gouting as high as the deck. The swells – which might have been expected to steepen in the coastal shallows – were killed stone dead, crushed by the weight. One minute *Kylie* was rolling through twenty degrees and doing four knots, and the next she was lying still, quivering beneath tons of water which thundered onto the deck, gushed from the scuppers or cascaded over the toe rail to disappear among a mass of brawling spears. It was impossible to know where the air ended and the sea began. My pipe clattered across the bridge deck but I did not scramble after it. A violin was screeching inside my head and all sense of direction had gone. Up was still up and down was down but north could be just about anywhere. Before the rainstorm started *Kylie* had been heading south-west for the sea-buoy off Livingston but I had been glancing only now and then at the compass, preferring to hold the course by keeping the wind on my left cheek. Now there was no wind to fan anything, or star or compass to steer by. *Kylie* was in a cylinder of sound and fury, lit by ghastly lightning, and in her cockpit a bristly black boar was jigging on the compass.

. . . which is not the same, of course, as making love, I added when the rain stopped and my breathing was near normal, *though nobody these days seems at all inclined to say so . . .*

The engine dot-and-carried *Kylie* up the Rio Dulce gorge in utter calm, with me keeping my better ear open for some reply, or – if speech were not possible – a sign my thoughts had got through. Was the ripple on the starboard bow the dive of a cormorant, or was Pip asking about the clinic? Could the distant shimmer on El Golfete be coming from a source brighter than the sun? I longed to know.

For months after the deluge I was as often making notes about people as about boats. The notes were not parts of a diary, nor were they written with the aim of exploring relationships. Rather, they were recollections of words spoken by a few men to – or about – a few women, and they lie among jottings about the cheapness of Guatemalan bus fares, the pros and cons of foresail furling-gear and the immensity of beefsteaks in the Rocky Mountains. Not having heard more than the odd word from Pip for more than a year, it's as if I were asking how well or badly other wives and husbands communicated with each other in the hope of finding out what was frustrating my efforts to get in touch with mine. ("Death, you fool!" not being an answer I could accept.) In calling them husbands and wives, I use the language loosely. And because the men were sailors, the wives had strong nautical connections.

"Oars," for example, said Jim, the owner of a 45-foot sloop, when I returned in a limp condition to Mario's that afternoon and we were waiting for Barrie to rewind a video. "I had a pair of beautiful oars, once. But a couple of years ago in the Bahamas I salvaged a big boat that had been blown ashore in a 50-knot gale. After I had refloated his boat I gave the skipper this beautiful pair of oars to help him get by. When he was shipshape again and ready to go on with his cruise, the girl who was crewing me packed her bag and told me she was sailing away with the other skipper, not with me. I said to the skipper, 'Bud, I saved your boat and I gave you my pair of lovely oars, but now, goddammit, you've not only got my oars but also my lovely woman as well. Keep my woman, Bud, but give me back my oars."

"Did he?"

"No, he sailed clear away with the both of them, but months later he came back aboard with the woman on one arm and a lovely pair of oars under the other. They weren't the originals, you understand, but the varnish on them was beautiful, and he gave them to me. Before they stepped ashore again the woman pulled me aside and said: 'Jim, it's not working out; I want to come back to you'. But I clipped those beautiful oars right back into my dinghy, and do you know what I said? 'Go away, woman,' I said. 'Oars I can use; you I can't.'"

At Mario's: Next week the Calders will sail for New Orleans. Am invited to go with them in *Nada* and on by car to Montana, where N. will write his cruising guide. Cannot turn this down; engine repairs will have to wait.

At Mañana marina a splenetic man who's been let down in a business deal is sounding off. "Those who can't stand the heat had better get out of the kitchen," he bellows at an upright woman sitting opposite, but from length of her fingernails it's not easy to picture her having hands-on experience of a cooker. He has large head on which sits small hat. Nobody tells him to shut up.

Tortured by old spinal injury, all afternoon Jimmie lies flat out on floor. "I need to get me a good woman," says he at sunset, so I tell him about lamp-trimmer from Aberdeen who in 1913 was paid off ship in Manchester during wakes week. Among festive crowd in beer tent he voices same need that J. has just expressed. Accompanied by pails of beer, sympathetic listeners take him by horse and cart to inspect what's on offer in neighbouring streets. At cost of fourteen gold sovereigns (£14 or $22.40), by midnight has become owner of two armchairs, brass firescreen, voluptuous widow and high-quality gladstone bag. With dawn and his awakening, he discovers armchairs are worm-eaten and widow has bad breath. Learning that another ship is paying off, returns with chattels to beer tent, where sells furniture for three half-crowns (39p or $62\frac{1}{2}$ c), attires widow in comely gown and auctions her off. She is knocked down to boatswain from Kent for £40 ($64) and the lamp-trimmer hies home to Aberdeen with gladstone bag.

Rigid with pain, J. doesn't smile.

"When I sailed with him in 1946 he was still using the gladstone bag," I add as J. crawls back to boat, but this doesn't raise smile, either. Should have pointed out significance of Aberdeen.

At Mario's: Letters from Laurence C. and Jane K. They want to come out to sail in *Kylie*. Together, impossible; separately, yes. Sew patch on ghoster where spreader has nicked it. Breakfast on what in USA are called English muffins. Aren't real muffins but sad fairy-cakes. Daphne agrees, " . . . but we couldn't call them that because they'd not sell." (Why ever not? Isn't bottom line dolours and scents?)

. . . a voluptuous widow and a Gladstone bag.

J., on vodka, suddenly vows to give me $10,000 (£6250). Is it the Smirnoff? Agree to travel Guatemala city and beyond with Wilbur, who owns fast-food outlets in New Hampshire.

Till yesterday *Kylie* was smallest cruiser for miles, but now Marc Hightower sails in in *Freebird*, a 21-footer from California. At upper end of scale is *Satori*, Alan Read's 50-plus-feet of cypress-wood elegance.

By bus to Antigua [Guatemala] with Wilbur. City is noted by guidebook for Easter processions but is noted by me as only city have ever come across that has no billboards and no McDonald's. Find their absence soothing, so Antigua becomes first city would willingly re-visit because of what it hasn't.

In evening Wilbur and self buy picture postcards of Antigua. Go through narrow doorway into back-street bar where we are sole customers. Windows blacked-out: no sight of passers-by. Wondering why, I settle down to write postcards. W. goes off to far table and shouts for service. Two girls patter out from shadows, unbutton shirts and sit on W's knees. Faces are nothing to write home about but turns out this doesn't matter because they sit with backs towards him so that breasts are easier to get at. Moaning softly, W. kneads and squeezes with frenzy of doughnut-filler who is running low on cream. No words exchanged – just gurgles and low moans. Appalled but fascinated, bend head over first postcard. Before have signed off and penned kisses, W. lets go of breasts and shouts for beer. Girls pad back into shadows, madam brings beers, W. shuffles to my table and at once is discussing artwork of postcards as though had been doing nothing else since coming in.

At Mario's: Returned p.m. with W. Transfer bags to *Nada* for passage to Lousiana. Having upped promised gift to $15,000 (£9375) while wishing me bon voyage, Jim promptly falls down steps and bloodies nose.

"Hear you had a problem in Antigua," says Daphne when am handing her *Kylie*'s key.

"Eh . . .?"

"Yes. With the girls . . . Seems you acted funny . . ."

"Funny . . .?"

"Yes, funny . . . As in queer."

"You know, I thought you might say that," I say.

In *Nada*, crossing Gulf of Mexico towards New Orleans: Leg of roast lamb and hot shower, so have no sensation of roughing it. Watching me shave, Pippin says "I'm glad girls don't have moustaches." Later, in response to Terrie's instruction to open maths books, she produces tears. In America in 1860s, Trollope was appalled by behaviour of its children. To him they seemed pampered tyrants, especially at mealtimes and on journeys. None of this in *Nada*, though. If commands or reasoning don't work, children are exiled to forecabin till agree to toe the line.

After lamb and roast potatoes, feels like Sunday afternoon and Pip and I will soon be going walk with dog. Instead, N. starts *Nada*'s engine and Terrie and I wash up. T. has not eaten. Though seas are slight, she feels sick. To T. sea passages are unavoidable entry fee to delights of foreign lands.

At Bridger, Montana. October: N. and I take turns about on word-processor. During daytime he writes 2000 words for publication in cruising guide and between supper and bedtime I write perhaps 200 for publication by nobody. I envy him his ability to harvest and winnow vast amounts of grainy detail.

Teachers at Bridger Junior High School donate nearly-new books with parallel Spanish-English texts, for Up and Down. Pack 30 into two cartons and picture them going on horseback down Old Spanish Trail and Pan-American Highway to La Ceiba and on by *cayuco* to Up and Down, but really they will go by air-conditioned truck and diesel-electric container ship.

Jane will fly out to Guatemala; Laurence C. will meet me in Honduras later.

In *Nada*, December: New Orleans towards Isla Mujeres [Isle of Women, off NE Yucatán]: Set off for sea down 100 miles of Mississippi instead of usual canal. By midnight have made 46 miles in $5\frac{1}{2}$ hrs against $2\frac{1}{2}$-knot current. Main hazards are oncoming tugboats pushing barges. To cheat current they take bends on inside lane, sometimes passing us to starboard instead of to port.

At 3 in the morning N. and I are in cockpit. Technically N. is off-watch, but he remains in cockpit, dozing. T. and children asleep below deck and I am steering. See lights of an oncoming vessel 3 miles ahead. Are not lights of vessel towing or pushing but of power-driven craft under way, so alter course to starboard as per international rules. When oncoming mastlights have moved out of line and green light is fainter I return *Nada* to her former course. After couple of minutes, oncoming boat alters course towards me, bringing his mastlights into line again and both sidelights as bright as before. Again I alter course, but 30° this time so that for a while he sees only *Nada*'s red sidelight and white mastlight. My intention to pass him on my port hand should now be plain and clear. When *Nada* is within 100 yds of riverbank I go back to former course, but yet again other boat brings his mastlights in line to head straight for me. What should I do? There's half a mile of clear water to port, but if I steer to port, likely as not he will choose same moment to alter course to his starboard and there'll be a collision. I ease back the engine revs and hold my course.

Seconds later three jarring crashes come from below. *Nada* has run onto a revetment.

Some wounds never heal. It is now six years since I wrote the notes about it and still I cover my eyes when I think of what Nigel and Terrie went through because of my wrong judgement. To describe in detail how they saved their boat would be painless if I hadn't been the author of the disaster. All I can say is that they launched the dinghy, loaded it with an an anchor and warp, motored off into the darkness, laid the anchor across the current and, in the space of half an hour or so, hauled *Nada* off the rocks and had her afloat. They worked together at launching the dinghy without help from me. I worked apart, at the stern, unclamping the dinghy's outboard motor from the rail, decanting petrol into its tank and handing it down to them in the dinghy.

Why did I do so little? I wasn't paralysed by shock, so why didn't I turn to and help launch the dinghy? Here the writing gets more difficult.

I couldn't work as quickly as they could, and thought that any intervention would slow them down. In the day-to-day running of the boat our having different work-rates hadn't mattered. Nigel's ability to tie seven reef-knots in the time I took to tie five, for example, meant only that the awning was rigged a few seconds later than it would otherwise have been if Terrie had been helping him. But in this emergency, good teamwork could mean the difference between living and dying. Terrie and Nigel were so used to working together that they had achieved a level of competence in handling the gear which I could not match. I wasn't downright clumsy, but I never became any better at doing these things than middling fair. At the anchorages where I'd helped him launch the dinghy during the passage north Nigel had had to shout "Hup-away backwards" and similar orders as many times at the fourth launching as at the first. When Terrie had teamed with him he'd called fewer directives and the launchings had gone more smoothly. Another thing, too: the previous launchings had been done in daylight; this was being done in darkness. Then, I'd been able to see his lips; now, many of his words would be lost.

This does not quite let (or get) me off the hook. I may not have been able to let go the lashings as quickly as Nigel could, or readily remember the angle at which the dinghy should be tilted after lifting it from its chocks so that its keel didn't foul the mainboom, but surely I could have helped Terrie to lift the dinghy over the guardrail? I thought not. I reckoned that I'd have upset their teamwork; I'd have mis-heard their orders; the launching would have been hindered.

It is not difficult to imagine the thoughts which must have filled Nigel's mind when he was jolted awake by the impact of the keel on the rocks. What sticks in my mind is that he straightaway jumped up onto the coachroof and set about unlashing the dinghy. Not a word was said. If I'd have been he, the decent veil of night would've been ripped by a sharp oath.

Nada put out to sea from the South Pass of the Mississippi at daybreak with Nigel at the tiller.

13

Good Friday in Guatemala

A strong Norther carried *Nada* quickly south-eastwards across the Gulf. After re-visiting anchorages on the coast of Yucatán and Belize, she was back at Mario's in the last week of Lent. With camera and artist's brushes, the Calders set off for the interior again to record the dreadful heaviness of Mayan ruins. Still in its North American school uniform, the bus trundled across the bridge over the Rio Dulce and disappeared in a blue haze. I asked around for a mechanic who could repair *Kylie*'s engine.

"Yup, I'll fix it," said a man whose face I could not quite place.

We rummaged through the spare parts that I'd brought out from England.

"D'you know this model of engine well?"

"Yup."

Yes, but the face did not quite match up with the hat. Was he, I wondered, the cowhand at the corner table who ducks for cover whenever John Wayne walks in . . .?

"How long will it take, d'you think . . .?"

"One week."

I loaded my camera and boarded the next bus. Lent would soon be over, but by travelling all day I could get to Antigua in time to see the processions of Semana Santa.

When I got back to Mario's at the end of Holy Week Jane would have flown out from England, *Kylie*'s battery would have been filled with lovely amps and soon afterwards I could be at sea, sailing to the Bay Islands with a pretty companion.

The bus was short-bodied, painted blue. I sat next to an open window. An Indian woman passed me up sliced melon. I bit into it and was filled with the happy thought that by Saturday week Jane and I would be in the Gulf of Honduras in *Kylie*.

Not till the bridge was a mile behind me did I recollect where it was that I had seen the mechanic before. He had been sitting at a table in a too-small hat, shouting about what people in kitchens should do if they couldn't stand the heat.

I wiped my face with a spotted red handkerchief and leaned back in my seat.

Not many able-bodied Guatemalan men in Antigua leaned backwards and closed their eyes on that Thursday evening. After sunset families came onto its cobbled streets to make carpets of sawdust or of flowers and leaves outside their front doors. The most vividly colourful were of sawdust; sackfuls of it poured into wooden formers laid on top of the cobbles. The sawdust had been dyed in a range of brilliant colours, from carmine through deep marigold and green to electric blue. Throughout the night fathers and sons tamped down the sawdust with small rakes. Past them in the early hours padded sinister figures in black-and-purple gowns. The carpetmakers ignored them, stopping work only to smoke and drink, so that when the sun rose above the mountains on Good Friday its beams slanted between the houses into streets carpeted with vivid pictures of birds and flowers.

I watched them trickling a sawdust tail for a scarlet macaw on a field of blue.

"Pharisees and Sadducees," said a Princess Margaret figure before raising a camera at a hooded man who was tying his shoelace.

By sunrise the narrow sidewalks were murmurous; at six-thirty the church squares were densely thronged. I edged through a conclave of Pharisees, set my camera at f5.6, focused it on a Roman soldier on a white charger who was tightening the chin-strap of his helmet, and pressed the button. Before I could frame a second shot Princess Margaret had come between two Sadducees and stood herself in front of me. She was joined by her Lady-in-Waiting, who set up a tripod and mounted a Leica on it. By this time the upper walls of the church were bathed in sunshine. I altered the setting of my camera to f11 and shifted to the women's left.

There came the beat of a drum. Princess Margaret stubbed out a cigarette, the Sadducees closed ranks and a Roman soldier looked at his wristwatch.

Longer than a London bus, borne on eighty shoulders, a catafalque of Christ on the road to Calvary emerged from the church. His head was as tall as the church portals and the cross was higher. Piloted by a elderly Sadducee in sunglasses, the catafalque wound through streets lined with Pharisees and Roman soldiers, through air darkened by smoke and heavy with incense. The drum thudding a slow heartbeat, the armour-plated cavalry, Pontius Pilate haggard, two thieves in chains, and behind them the catafalque.

But the message it was sending out was different from the one I was taking in. The Christ was a plaster figure too high above me to easily focus on, so my camera zoomed in on the present imperfect rather than the past historic, on the Roman soldier's wristwatch and the High Priest's sunglasses, but not the plaster figure.

"That Pilate chap runs a hardware store," confided the Lady-in-Waiting; "but the most fascinating thing is that Barabas is doing time in the local clink for robbery with violence."

I didn't need to know those details; if recent Guatemalan history was anything to go by, before this Easter was long over the death squads would be out in their white vans looking for another discontented carpenter.

The catafalque wound through the twisting streets with the slowness of a blood clot on its way to the brain. By evening the sawdust carpets had been trampled to mush and Princess Margaret was on her way to the Ritz Continental in a hired car.

The blue bus which took me back to Guatemala city broke down at a dusty crossroads where a newly made pinewood bench and chest of drawers were being offered for sale by a long-faced carpenter in a bib-and-brace overall. I pulled open a drawer and saw that, instead of mortised joints, the corners had been nailed and glued.

The bus crawled through a shantytown into the city, and soon afterwards Jane was threading through the clutch of porters at the airport carrying a green-and-grey rucksack and a saxophone in a black case. She was a woman now, but to me she was still the bright-eyed child I had known since her birth.

"I really do need this holiday," said Jane. "I really do need to get spaced out."

"The Bay Islands will be just the ticket!"

When we got back to Mario's we found the engine in pieces. The mechanic was nowhere to be seen.

"He got a last-minute charter for his boat," said Barrie, "so he's taken off for Belize."

Jane and I sat in *Kylie*'s cabin, watching the rain. We had filled a few days agreeably, but we knew that by the time the engine could be repaired her holiday would have trickled away.

In a bar that night she played her saxophone with a local group. After half an hour of warm work she came over to me and said "I'm really thirsty, Peter. What'll I have?"

"Mineral water, of course. It'll be a good chance for you to practise your Spanish. Go on; ask for an *agua minerale sin gaz*."

"Peter, *please* don't tell me what to do."

Next day we arranged for her to go as crew aboard an American boat which was leaving for Belize and the USA.

"Damn that mechanic, Jane, " I told her. "We needed to get to sea."

14

The Venus Delivery

On the day Jane handed the saxophone over *Kylie*'s guardrail and was
borne downriver with it to Amatique Bay, Alan Read asked me to go
aboard *Satori* for a nightcap. The invitation brought a wobble to my
gin. Till then Alan had kept aloof, anchoring *Satori* a full mile from
the marina and dinghying ashore to Mario's only twice a week. Looked
at from *Kylie*'s sweltering cockpit, his situation was better by far. The
thatched lounge-bar of the marina was cool and airy, and in windy
weather gave good shelter to *Kylie* nestled in its lee, but when the
breezes fell light the temperature of my cabin rose to the middle
nineties. If the mechanic had not said he needed my boat to be on a
jetty, *Kylie* would have been anchored out on the river too, for *Satori*'s
cabins were cooled by the lightest breezes and she lay far enough away
from the bank to avoid many of the insects which found their way
though the mosquito nets into *Kylie*'s cabin to be bludgeoned to death
by Little Miss Muffet. Then, overnight, *Satori* had weighed anchor and
come into Mario's, berthing only yards away from *Kylie*, the curve of
her elegant sheerline lost among a clutter of smaller boats, and her
cabins as hot as mine.

In the lamplight Alan's beard gleamed ginger at its edges but his face
was lined and tense. He poured a 1989 Kentucky whiskey into a 1920
Birmingham silverware cup, which I raised presently to toast his
health.

"Hold on!" he said, swatting at a mosquito.

"That was quick!"

He rubbed the blood smear from his palm and scowled.

"Why didn't you stay out on the river? There'd be breezes all night
long – and fewer horrors to bite you."

"No way! Some things out on the river can take your hand off."

"Well, *you* should know," I said.

"I'll murder them," he growled into his cup.

"Ah," I said, thinking that he probably would. Though softly spoken,

Alan was all sinew and hard knuckle.

"Bastards!"

"Don't let them eat you," I said; but the whiskey was half gone before he managed a small smile, and even that was tight and grim.

No wonder.

One night while I had been away in Antigua (had reported Daphne), Alan had dinghied up-river to a lakeside diner. Returning aboard at midnight he had come across some robbers. Before he could get to grips with them they had slithered into a motorized *cayuco* and roared off. Armed with only a flashlight, he had leapt into his dinghy and in a very few minutes had caught up with two fleeing Indians and was yelling at the helmsman to stop. In response, one of the Indians had struck out at him with a machete. The blow had dashed the flashlight from Alan's grasp and the robbers had escaped.

He opened up his palm to the cabin lamplight and glared at it.

"Bastards," he said again, studying his lifeline.

The whiskey bottle emptied, I swung down from *Satori*'s sterndeck on to the marina walkway. Marc Hightower came down from the bar, where he had been talking to Daphne, and stood at the top of the steps. He was not so tall as Alan but had a squarer face, longer hair and a wider smile.

"How's the engine repair going?"

"It isn't. He won't be back for another week, Daphne says."

"Too bad."

"Yes. I'd like to get sailing."

"So how about coming on a delivery from Venezuela with me and Alan?"

"With Alan? But what about *Satori*? Why would he want to leave her?"

"Seven hundred dollars, plus expenses."

I slapped my wrist quickly but too late: the mosquito had been and gone. I rubbed at the puncture and buttoned my sleeve.

"I don't know, Marc . . . Let me think about it."

Why does the grass on the other side always look greener? Seven hundred dollars was not an offer to turn down lightly but the certain prospect of getting to sea at last was the main reason why half an hour later I told Marc I'd go with him. The job sounded straightforward. We were to sail a 35-foot cruiser-racer from Tucacas in Venezuela and deliver it to Mario's, 1300 miles across the Caribbean to the west. The tradewind and the North Equatorial current would be coming from well

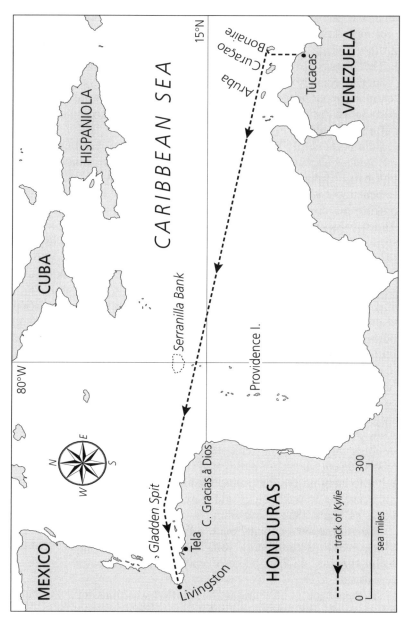

Chart 6: Caribbean Sea: Tucacas, Venezuela to
Livingston, Guatemala.

abaft the beam all the way, so we might cover the distance in under nine days – time enough, I thought, for the mechanic to have repaired *Kylie*'s engine.

The owner had said the delivery boat was in good condition. "Rafaelo seems to be a nice guy, a straight guy, but he doesn't know too much about boats," said Marc. "She's twenty years old and hasn't been sailed for months, so there'll be quite a few days' work to do before she's ready."

Courteous, wittily laconic, Rafaelo did not stint on spending dollars. At Caracas airport he hired a gleaming black vehicle which sported bull-bars, opulent armchairs which swivelled at will, and opaque, impenetrable windows. Alan and I reclined grandly in the armchairs, puffing his cigarettes and pretending we weren't at all impressed. Tyres screeching on bends and the crew swivelling to suit, Rafaelo sped us through a neon-lit city and on through the black night towards the coast. What with his stylish driving, the smoky windows and the recliners, we could have been Mafiosi on their way to winkle out a pearl.

Rafaelo's boat turned out not to be an oyster however but a wrinkled seahorse which had slalomed round race-buoys in its youth and had borne off some plumpish trophies in its heyday, but which, by the time we boarded her in Tucacas, had acquired more than a few stretch-marks to show for her winning ways. We scrutinised the hull and rigging from masthead to keel. In the place where a pearl would have lain in an oyster we found a discoloured hexagonal nut. Alan fingered it and wagged his head.

"It was laying in the bilge," he said gloomily, "so you need to put a double query next to the keelbolts."

We dug out a length of plasticated chain of the sort used for tethering bikes to lamp-posts. "Two ten-pound anchors shackled to this stuff is all we've got to hold us . . . and the chain jams solid in a navel pipe that's no bigger than a sink drain."

Marc uncapped a pen and made a list. "No reefing pendants . . . no safety lines . . . frozen boom fittings . . . rotted forward hatch . . . slack lower shrouds . . . That makes twenty-two jobs, all of them more or less urgent."

"Is there time . . .?" I began, but really I was thinking: "The deck gear is rotten; we ought to cry off."

Marc re-capped his pen. "I'm contracted to deliver this boat," he said, "so let's do it."

Marc and Alan worked on the engine and electronics while I worked away on the sails and rigging with a splicing-fid, palm and needle. In six days we had made good eighteen of the twenty-two faults and were impatient to be off and away. On the eve of the seventh we patted our handiwork and told ourselves that things were at last looking quite shipshape. On deck we now had a brand-new autopilot, robust jack-stays from pulpit to each quarter and reefing-gear on the mainsail; below deck a healthy-sounding engine pumped amps into a bank of new batteries and a pair of Alan's hand-crafted pot-holders gleamed in the galley. In addition to the basics, our higher needs had been catered for too, said Marc with a wide smile, for Rafaelo had supplied us with a boxful of taped music: reggae for them and Beethoven for me. Over de-frozen lobster and a bottle of Chianti, we agreed that the boat was as ready for sea as we could reasonably make it. It didn't matter too much that there was no radio to receive weather forecasts, that the speed-and-distance log did not work and that the wire cable on the steering gear was the wrong sort . . .

Mark swallowed Chianti and frowned at the lobster. "Have we got backups in the doubtful areas? How about weather forecasts?"

"Won't be a big problem: keep an eye on the sky, record the barometer every two hours, talk to passing ships . . .?"

"No VDO for speed and distance, so what about DR positions..?"

"Shan't need them – we've got the satnav and the sextant."

"Steering gear? That one-by-nineteen wire's not flexible enough."

"If it breaks we can use the emergency tiller . . .but how about getting, just in case, a dozen of those . . . whatdyoucallums? . . . bulldog grips?"

"Bulldog grips . . .? 'Cable clamps,' you mean."

Rafaelo roared in from Caracas to see us off, bringing six cases of beer and one of rum.

"What a man!" grinned Alan as we coiled the docklines.

The grin did not stay in place for long. An hour later, having motored down a tortuous channel to the sea, we began to make sail. I sweated on the halyard winch.

"More! The luff's not tight . . ."

My knuckles went whiter.

"Headboard's still a foot below the sheave. *More* . . .!"

Now the veins on the back of my hand were strangely purple. "Poh . . .! Pah . . .!" I puffed, heaving harder. The halyard parted with a agreeable twang and a quantity of mainsail fell about his ears.

In the lee of a sandy cay we tried to repair the halyard, but it proved to be sun-rotted. Knotting a narrow blue bandanna about his head, Marc said we would go on to Bonaire, 80 miles distant, using the topping-lift as a halyard.

We weighed anchor and headed out, motoring gingerly past a reef because the depthsounder had stopped working. Alan stood like a black statue in the bows, shining a mini-searchlight into the water and calling out the changing character of the sea-bed as we went. At the wheel Marc's fingers were twitching with anger. At first I put it down to the fact that an hour earlier I had rattled cutlery and broken sharply into his sleep, but when later that night we were safely clear of the reefs in deep water and the signs of anger were still twitching in his face, I began to think that perhaps worse matters than rattling teaspoons were putting him in such bad temper. Was it Alan and me who were at fault, or was it the boat? In addition to the rotten main halyard and the no-good depthsounder, perhaps the boat had other shortcomings which he had not let on about? I didn't know. All I knew was that we could be in deep trouble later on in the passage if the skipper was in bad mood at its start.

I told him of my misgivings during the morning watch, when we were reaching across a fifteen-knot wind towards Bonaire, now a dark smudge on the horizon ahead. From time to time a sea broke against the quarter, knocking the boat's head twenty degrees off the course. Marc put his hand on the auto-pilot's servo-motor and pulled a face.

"Aw! It's overloaded; it can't cope."

"That the only problem?"

"What d'you mean? What's on your mind?"

Putting aside the thought that if the main halyard had broken in ten knots of wind others might very well fall apart when it blew harder, I began with us, the crew. It was going to be difficult enough for three habitually solo sailors as opinionated as we were to rub along happily in the same boat, especially as, owing to the Chianti, all of us now knew that I was a Libran, that Alan had been born under Scorpio and that Marc himself was a Sagittarian. Was there, did he think, an awful misalliance in our stars? In particular, was he satisfied with my doings? How did I rate, for instance, at darning? And then there was the small matter of the logbook. We ought to keep a more detailed record. Not just now-and-then notes of our course but of everything that we did. If any damage happened to the boat, the logbook would be the first thing the bloody insurers would ask for. Indeed, if the worst came to the worst, I said, with the gloomy relish of the born-again bank clerk, the logbook would be the only way to protect Rafaelo's chequebook.

He heard me out in silence. "Right! From now on, at every change of watch we'll enter the satnav read-out, course and distance made good, barometer, and all that. Then if the satnav breaks down we've at least got an upgraded position to help with your navigation."

"My navigation?"

"I didn't ask you to come along to darn sails – I was thinking about your fancy navigation as well. You'd better keep your sextant dusted, because maybe the satnav will go down next . . ."

As he spoke, a wave hit the quarter. The autopilot screamed, the wheel spun, and a series of twangs and bangs came from under the cockpit. The steering cable had parted. Unfortunately, we had not been able to find any bulldog grips in the local hardware store before we'd left . . .

Alan bolted the six-foot emergency tiller onto the head of the rudder stock and steered the course for Bonaire. It was difficult work. To clear the compass pedestal the tiller had to be canted upwards at a forty-five-degree angle, so depriving the helmsman of most of its mechanical advantage. Although the seas were only moderate our arms and shoulders could stand only twenty-minute spells before we were wincing.

At Bonaire Marc went ashore to buy swages and wire, leaving me to eat ice-cream with the First Mate of a general-cargo boat. These days, said the Mate in between licks of a chocolate cornet with cream topping, 8000-tonners carried no Radio Officer and only two Mates and three Able Seamen. They had no lookout except the officer on watch, and the navigation was done by satellite navigator, autopilot and radar, never by sextant.

Vanilla ice-cream dripped onto my khaki shorts while he was telling me these details. In my day, I hissed back at him, 8000-tonners had carried a crew of forty-seven and gone about their business with lookout and lead.

Marc came back aboard accompanied by a sad-eyed, middle-aged man with a drooping moustache and a white yachting cap. Tipping back the cap, Ishmael announced that he was the father of four strapping children and the rigger of quite a few large and famous sailboats. He squatted on the foredeck, separated a length of 6 x 19 wire into its component strands and set about making a no-fail wire-to-rope splice in a new halyard. After half an hour of weaving the strands over, across, down-between and under-up each other, he held up a mare's-tail for our inspection.

"Go away, Ishmael; I c'n do better myself," muttered Marc, and soon his first rope-to-wire splice was thrumming against the mast, undergoing a winch test. To inject a matching air of confidence into the navigation department, I dusted the sextant and scanned the sky. High above the island hung Arcturus, but Castor and Pollux were too low to be useful. I turned my head westward.

"Good Lor'!"

"What's wrong?" said Alan, bent over my watch on the chart table, waiting for me to cry "Hup!"

"I've found the root of our problems. Come out and take a look! You'll have seen nothing like it in your life."

The planets Mars, Jupiter and Venus were blazing in Cancer. Their brightness outshone any star's but it was not their brilliance that was remarkable; what was disturbing was the closeness of each planet to the other. No doubt about it: we were were about to witness a three-part astronomical conjunction of a magnitude which in times past had turned pot-makers into pilgrims. Not having been so intimate with each other for a hundred years or so, it was as if the three planets were bent on having an orgy. Red with desire, Mars was lusting towards Venus, but at his shoulder Jupiter was panting after her, too. I put down the sextant and groped for my tobacco. No creature now alive had ever seen a copulation of such immensity; nor could anyone predict reliably its outcome. The heavenly conjunction might not be so serious if only a couple of deities were going to be at it, but *three* of them spending a long week-end in the same Zodiacal bed could have consequences which mortals might find upsetting. Questions like "Did the earth move, darling?" would have to be taken literally for once, and the television screen would be filled twice nightly with Patrick Moore.

For the number 3 was the sum of 1 and 2, and was the first number to join the odd with the even, so it possessed super-magical powers. Sometimes the magic could perhaps be benign, but – as we very well knew – more often it was malignant: the breaking of the halyard and the collapse of the steering gear might be only the beginning of a long catalogue of disasters. What further interventions into our little lives did the mighty planets have in mind? Would they toss three coins in the fountain and invite us to make wishes, or would they hurl us into the clutches of three witches?

It did not take long to find out which way their intentions lay. Next afternoon the wind blew at 30 knots, raising large whitecaps in the strait between the anchorage and the smaller island of Klein Bonaire. Two yachts struggled in from the west, their mainsails torn and engines silenced by heavy seas. Marc and Alan talked-in the stricken boats by radio.

"Huh! We'll lie doggo till this hooley goes down a bit," said Marc, sticking an anti-seasickness patch behind his right ear. "The forecast says it'll blow over during the night, so we'll not leave till early tomorrow. Then, if we have any more breakages, we'll be able to put into Curaçao for repairs while it's still daylight."

"I'll cook a big dinner," I said. "How about fried chicken breasts and these . . . cucumber whatsits?"

"Cucumbers . . .? You mean zucchinis."

"Beg pardon? Say it again, please," I said, fixing my eyes on his lips.

"Zucchinis," repeated Marc with his uncensorious smile.

"*Sutteenie* . . .?"

"No, Peter. Listen . . .! Take it easy . . .! Say:'*Tsuk* . . .'"

"Suck . . .?"

Behind me, Alan thumped his fist on the chart table and snorted.

"What's up with *you*, then? I've never even *seen* the blessed things till now!"

"Not seen zucchinis . . .? Nor a coolbox with dry ice? Don't tell me you never saw dry ice?"

"As it happens, I haven't. But I do know the difference between a hotdog and a sausage."

"There isn't none."

"Course there bloody well is! A sausage is a sausage whatever temperature it's at, but a hotdog is only ever a newly-cooked one."

"Not where I come from it isn't," said Alan, stumping out to the cockpit to look daggers at the water.

"He's mad keen about fishing. He's laid off a course to the Serranilla Bank in hopes of catching bonito," growled Marc, still smiling; "but – shh! don't let on, will you? – we're not going to stop there . . .!

Bonaire disappeared behind us in a twenty-five-knot wind as we put up a double-reefed main and much-cut-down foresail. Even then, the boat yawed wildly, and so we rolled up the headsail and set *Kylie*'s little storm-jib in its place. Marc listened to the whirring of the autopilot and said: "That's better; things are easier for it now. We got to look after that baby 'cos if it goes sick we'll have to hand-steer for a thousand miles."

Behind a thin veil of cloud the planets watched and waited. As soon as the islands of Curaçao and Aruba had fallen abaft the beam out of easy reach, they stealthily uncoupled the propeller shaft from the engine and slid it out of the hull. It was as if a water main had burst in the cabin. In less than ten seconds Alan had jammed a wooden plug into the hole; five hefty blows from his hammer and the inrush of water had stopped. Before the propeller and its shaft had come to rest on the seabed two miles beneath us, Marc had pumped the bilge dry.

Twelve hours after that unhelpful incident, the hull was surfing down fifteen-foot swells when the autopilot let out a high scream and stripped its gears, and so from that moment onwards we had to steer all the while by hand. On a boat such as *Kylie* with a moderately long keel, steering downwind is quite tiring, but here it was exhausting. The mental concentration and physical energy needed to keep the skittish, fin-keeled racing hull on course meant that at the end of a two-hour trick at the wheel we went to our berths with clawed fingers, aching shoulders and addled brains.

The berths were deep and soft, but Marc and Alan found little rest in them because the powers of the anti-seasickness patches did not match the promises on the labels. For so long as the weather stayed rough, Marc and Alan ate only dry biscuits and slept little. And, getting at me evening after evening, whenever I took over the wheel Alan would laugh in my face and say: "You won't need the compass – just keep pointin' at Venus."

"Oh, really?" I felt like saying back. "Oh *yeah*, old chap?" Just *pointing* at Venus was, perhaps, all right. So long as the gesture looked like a salute we might pass muster, but mock her, laddie, and she'd get shirty. For Venus was also Ishtar, the all-powerful goddess of the Egyptians; and she was Frigg, wife of Odin, chief god of the northern pantheon . . . So just you bear in mind those terrible titles, chum! Be respectful. Doff your cap and touch your forelock. Keep the boat running towards Venus, by all means, but don't – whatever you do – run her down. And no matter what happens, boyo, don't start singing that little ditty about a good ship of the same name, whose figurehead was a whore in bed . . .

The winds eased, the stresses on the creaking hull and its worn gear became less, and Marc and Alan rapidly perked up. Believing we had escaped the wrath of the planets, I set about making a beef stew.

"Music, Marc? How about a bit of *Pastoral Symphony*?"

"Sorry! We only have reggae."

"That's disgraceful! You said that Rafaelo had put some Beethoven aboard. You don't deserve any dessert."

"What sort d'you have in mind?"

"Something special: tinned rice pudding, laced with Aunt Jemima Original Maple Syrup."

"Shit!" said Marc cheerfully, coming down from the cockpit clutching his toothbrush. "Couple o' days ago I thought we weren't going to make it. When we started surfing I found myself thrown forward over the wheel, looking down into a trough and thinking, 'Jeeze! If we pitchpole, the mast is going overboard and we'll open up like a Coke can'."

"Why's that?"

"You noticed the sidedecks? They bulge an inch upwards at the shroud plates. And you seen the way the deck caves in at the heel of the mast?" He glanced outside and chuckled. Bright as a five-mile flare, Venus was shining through the poled-out genoa. "It's not the planets that are bugging us! Our problems come from human beings stressing materials beyond their limits an' neglecting to repair them."

Alan waggled a beer at the planets and nodded. "That little Venus number," he seemed to say, "doesn't know her ass from her elbow . . ."

Two hours after eating a plateful of my stew Alan was struck down by a sudden illness which left him pale, weak and breathless.

"What's hit me?" he croaked from the cockpit. "I haven't the strength to turn the wheel."

He crawled into the forward berth, cold and shaking. I hurried to make an entry in the log. I could not put his illness down to rough seas or the after-effects of my cookery however, for both Marc and I still felt quite hale, if not entirely hearty. Malaria? Meningitis? Mumps? So sudden and debilitating was Alan's illness that Marc laid off a course for the nearest doctor, on Providence island, 150 miles to the southwest. Alan lay all night in his bunk, shivering under blankets.

Like a distant comet, across the back of my mind passed the thought that his tubes might be blocked.

15

Dawn Rescue

Brighter than before, Venus crackled in the western sky, lasering into my brain. When daylight came, the image was still glowing there.

Dazed and drained, Alan struggled out into the cockpit, tugging on his jacket against a brisk wind.

"How're you feeling this fine morning?"

"Not so bad, now. Hell, I can't work out what caused it, though. It was like as if my whole body was filled with dry ice. Heck, it's a mystery.!"

"Yeah, it's a mystery," said Marc lightly, Venus being now out of sight below the horizon, over the Pacific. In the strengthening wind he crawled out on the boom to reeve a clew pendant ready to take in a second reef. Next thing we knew, the topping-lift swivel had torn out of the boom, the boom had dropped into the sea and Marc was plunged into six-foot waves.

"Keep her running!" he screamed, his trunk and legs dragging at six miles an hour through water of density 1023 kg per cm^3, adding another 24kgs to the forces which were gently prising his fingers from the boom. Alan lurched groggily to the guardrail and leaned far outboard.

"Don't luff up!" Marc screeched. "Keep the wind in the sail."

Now Alan's left hand was six feet along the boom, and Marc had dragged his legs up and was hooking them round the boom-end, but his hips were still underwater. A wave thudded against the stern. I put on half a turn of port wheel and hauled in a couple of yards of sheet. Alan's hand was no farther along the boom, but Marc was pulling himself inboard hand-over-hand by the reef pendants, into the bunt of the sail. I pulled in more sheet and steered ten degrees to starboard. Alan's hand clamped onto Marc's wrist and seconds later he had both feet on deck and, working together, he and Alan were tying the reef points.

"Huh!" said Marc when they had finished. "Good job those guys missed you with their machete."

That evening Jupiter shouldered Mars aside and nuzzled up to Venus. Now, I thought, perhaps she will be satisfied; having slapped down Marc and Alan, perhaps she will let us go our way in peace.

We ran on towards Guatemala, leaving far behind the reefs that lie northward of Cabo Gracias à Dios, the big knee of land at the eastern end of the Gulf of Honduras. The seas moderated, and so I fried a dinner of ham-dipped-in-batter, serving it with chipped potatoes.

"Any more French fries going?"

"Watch it! These here aren't French fries; they're genuine English chips," I said, passing out Alan's plate.

Next day bonito came after Alan's lure, and then tuna. Marc and I lifted the coolbox into the cockpit and tipped overboard a quantity of none-too-fragrant zucchinis, while Alan plied his rod. In minutes he had gaffed a forty-pounder and was cutting it up in the cockpit. At noon, having carried us westward 1090 miles from Bonaire in 8 days 7 hours, the wind eased to a gentle breeze.

Alan pegged open the forehatch and hung out his jacket in the rigging. With only 150 miles still to go, the passage was drawing to its close. I turned another page of the almanac: at last we were moving out of the influence of Venus. According to the predictions, our troubles were as good as over.

Then the new moon appeared a whole day earlier than the almanac said it would.

The conjunction of the three planets had amazed me, but this latest happening was incredible. The almanac had been accurate in forecasting the coming-together of the planets, but it seemed to have slipped up about the moon. I rubbed the image of Venus from my eyes and looked upwards again. The moon was certainly in the sky: a silver hair on a background of indigo silk: tomorrow's moon shining today.

"Turn over your pennies!" I called down the companionway, but they were dozing.

"We'll be back at Mario's by Saturday . . .," we told ourselves at nine that night whilst sinking our forks into Alan's tuna steaks which he'd grilled in butter and topped with caper sauce. " . . . back to loads of fresh water, Daphne's English muffins and dollars in our pockets. No more aching shoulders and split fingers for a while! No more putting up with ignorant oafs who coil ropes the wrong way round, can't set anchors in the way that I do, don't know the difference between a sausage and a hotdog, mis-apply magnetic variation and always manage to rattle the teaspoons when they wash up . . ."

We tilted Rafaelo's wonderful rum into our coffees and beamed warmly at each other across the cabin table and into the cockpit where our loyal shipmate was ungluing his fingers from the wheel.

"Lovely sauce that was, Alan."

"You did a neat job sewing the bimini."

"Beta double-plus for the logistics, Marc; Rafaelo chose lucky."

An hour before daybreak on the final day Marc came up into the cockpit to stand his watch. After allowing him the usual few minutes to get used to the darkness I unprised my fingers from the wheel, crawled into my berth and in seconds was drifting into sleep.

"On deck! On deck!"

The cries were not a part of a dream. Blinking, I blundered out of the companionway and stumbled to the binnacle. Marc was on the foredeck, fisting at the inboard end of the genoa pole.

"There, in the water!" he cried. "Luff up!"

"What is it? I see nothing!" The backs of the nearest seas were the sheen of old pewter and the troughs were dark scallops. But then I made out a darker patch of water that was not moving downwind like the rest of it.

"Men in the water! Tack round and head for them!"

I struggled to haul in miles of soggy mainsheet and head into the wind and, at the same time, get a sight of what he was pointing at, but the darkness was a whirl of flapping canvas, writhing lines, distracted fumbles and hoarse shouts.

I could hear a steady but urgent voice calling up other vessels for help on the cabin radio, but these words were mixed in with other cries about bastard Indians in *cayucos* and a flurry of sharp oaths. Then, above the furious clatter of the pole on the deck and the hoarse babble coming from the cabin, Marc thundered down at us from on high, "WE ARE GETTING THOSE MEN OUT OF THAT FUCKING SEA."

There were three of them, huddled on a capsized *cayuco*. I spun the wheel and played the mainsheet but missed them by yards on the first try. I botched the second attempt too, and our heaving-line tangled and fell short. A body flopped off the *cayuco*, thrashed through two yards of water, grabbed the line and was hauled aboard. At the third try I luffed up more neatly. Two other bodies were pulled up over the stern. They slumped into the cockpit, sodden, silent and shivering.

In the half-light the *cayuco* wallowed beneath our stern, two red canisters bobbing alongside it.

"Let's tow it," said Marc.

"Leave it, man, leave it!"

The speaker was a black man. His eyes were red, he was bleeding from a gash in the leg and his words were heavily slurred. "We don't want her no more . . . Jus' leave her, I'm telling you."

Marc was stern and gruff: "What about those canisters? What's in them?"

"Rice an' beans."

"No marijuana? Huh . . .? You *hearing* me . . .? You got any drugs on you?"

The black man pulled away a dreadlock from his cheek. "Hell, no. We had some in the boat, jus' enough for ourselves, you know? But we haven't got it no more . . . we lost it when the wave hit us."

We helped them below and boiled coffee. A huge banana-carrier in ballast glided silently near, silver-grey hull, registered in Bermuda, its maindeck fifty feet above the sea, rope ladder dangling over its side but not a single human being to be seen on it anywhere.

"What d'you think?" said Marc. "Shall we put them aboard?"

I looked at the cliff of steel, and at our masthead that was sawing at the clouds.

"If we roll against her sides the mast will come down."

So we gave them dry clothes and a hot meal and took them onward to Guatemala. Francisco, the eldest at about forty, was a middle-sized *mestizo* with an ordinary, comfortable face, the sort of face as likely to be seen in newsreel clips of Belfast or Birmingham as of Guatemala City. Xavier, called by them Alver, was a sharp-nosed youth who ate two platefuls of spaghetti bolognaise and then curled up like a cat in the forecabin and slept. Santos, the Black Carib, mainspring of the expedition, bloodied but unbowed, told us that they were conch-divers who had motored out from Tela in Honduras two nights previously, when the contest for Venus had been at its fiercest. Carrying ten days' food and water, they had set a course by the wind for Gladden Spit, on the barrier reef off Belize. For 1000 lempiras (£128 or $204.80) the *cayuco*'s owner had hired them the boat and an outboard engine, and provided fuel and food. The deal was that for every pound weight of conch they brought back to Tela he would give them two lempiras (26p or 42c). We raised our eyebrows at these figures; the fishermen would have needed to land a quarter of a ton of conch before they could clear their debt and start making a profit. It seemed a very poor deal indeed – and a rash one, too. Load a minimal half-ton of conch shells into that *cayuco* and its gunwales would be only inches above the water, said Alan, and Tela lay eighty miles distant from Gladden Spit, across the heaving waters of the Gulf. It seemed to us that Santos hadn't weighed these matters at all – or, if he had, had weighed them wrongly. He was forceful and muscular, and was at the time of life for chasing after rainbows. No matter that the *cayuco* had only inches of freeboard and no decking, or that the wind and seas would be coming at them broadside, it would be no problem! Santos had seen that same old sea lotsa times before! He *knew* it like nobody, man! At Gladden Spit they'd dive the reef all day, pick over their haul of shells in the sunset, then eat a little rice 'n fish, smoke a little pot, dream a little dream. Nothin' to it!

Santos shut his eyes, stroked his dreadlocks and went on talking. Twenty miles from land and beam-on to the seas, the *cayuco* had been rolled over by a large wave. The men had struggled to right their craft by first rocking it, then by lashing a stumpy pole to the hull and using it as lever. When neither attempt had succeeded, they had clung on to the overturned boat for twenty-two hours, burned by the sun by day, chilled by the wind at night and gnawed all the time by the fear that sharks would scent the blood oozing from their cuts.

Sharks didn't touch them at all, but despair did, coming in the night, worming into them after the bright lights of a steamer had passed by, less than a mile to the south. They had screamed and shouted at it, waved a paddle high above, but the steamer had ploughed past without stopping. Then a second pair of red and green lights had appeared, heading straight for them. Again they'd shouted, again waved the paddle in the gleam from the planets, but the ship hadn't stopped. Seeing the lighted cabins surging past him only a stone's-throw distant, Xavier had tried to throw himself into the water and swim towards them. By the time Santos had pinned him down and quietened him the ship had disappeared.

Alan fetched out a first-aid kit and bandaged his bleeding leg. I poured more coffee into his beaker.

But what *fools* they had been! Setting out in twenty-five knots of wind in such a boat! The Black Carib who had paddled his *cayuco* out of harbour on a calm night to voyage to Chachahuate, believing that not until mid-morning would there be any wind or waves to greatly hinder him, had taken a nicely calculated risk. Then, it had been ten chances to one in favour of the wind blowing no more than fifteen knots before he got to his earthly Paradise. His voyage had been risky, yes, but not crassly stupid. But *this*! Eighty miles! And six-foot seas coming from abeam! With an outboard motor and only one paddle!

"What's everybody's full names and dates of birth, Santos?" I said fussily. "I must write them down in the log."

He spat out a dreadlock and giggled. "Dates of our birthdays? Sweet Jesus! You a policeman?"

"For the moment, let's suppose that I am. There'll be real ones coming aboard in Livingston, you know . . ."

"I can just about tell you their *names*, I guess . . . but *dates*, no!"

"Well, let's make a start with yours, eh?"

"Santos Lambey. An' you can put me down as . . . uh . . . twenty-one."

"Yes, but what's your *date of birth*, Santos? The day, month and year?"

He shook his dreadlocks. "Uh-huh! I don't know them!"

I put down the pen, shut the logbook and went to the foredeck. Bobbing in the sunshine ahead of me lay the Rio Dulce buoy; we were almost home and dry. I lit my pipe.

But . . . but hadn't we too been foolish and wilfully blind? And weren't we too almost as deeply ignorant? For all the careful labour we had put into repairing its gear, we had set out in a boat that could easily have foundered, and though we knew our birthdates and our star-signs and had postcodes, though we could wire-up satnavs and work out our global position from the stars, what did we *really* know about the powers of Venus? Was it human error, and *nothing* else, that had landed us with those problems? And what about the influential input of the number 3? In the third boat to come along, three men had rescued three other men at their third try, after the coupling of three planets . . .

I took up the paddle, the only item of the fishing-expedition that remained. They had lost everything, while we – touch wood – would soon be putting dollars in our pockets. But these men, these fellow-fools and brother-sailors, were not returning to square one in Honduras; they had been knocked off the board, were out of the game . . .. That boatowner would be on their backs for ever!

"How're you feeling down below there, Santos?"

Santos smiled the wide, white, wonderful smile that only black people can produce.

"I'm happy, man, happy! We lost the boat, but we still got our lives." He took a plait of hair between his lips and sucked at it. "You know what? When I get ashore, I think I'll start goin' to church."

They gave me the paddle. I wiped the salt off the blade and wrote on it the date and, underneath it, "16° 14'N Latd. 87° 46'W Longd." . Then the three fishermen signed their names on the paddle, and below their signatures I printed "GRACIAS À DIOS", the name of the best-known cape nearest to where we had saved them from the sea.

The words were also the first words spoken by Santos when we had pulled him aboard. "Gracias à Dios," he had said to us: "thanks to God."

And the moon that night was a little larger.

Dawn rescue.

16
Fingers and Thumbs

The monkeys who had been trying to write *Hamlet* for as long as I could remember got down from their typewriters at twenty-two minutes past midnight and started on a concerto for two harps and a chainsaw. In spite of my swallowing a large white tablet, at three o'clock they were still at it. "You look a bit puffed."

"Too many fingers and thumbs . . .," said my pillow through the clamour, and so when daylight seeped into the cabin I raised the engine from its bed and lowered it, with a sigh, on to the jetty.

Minutes after I had done this the tall dark trees around me blazed with birds, and heavy night-clouds lifted from the hills to the south of the Rio Dulce. At that moment I understood how the stalwart Eric Newby had felt on giving up a career in women's mantles so as to climb a mountain in the Hindu Kush. I, too, felt an urge to fill the air with song.

Daphne came by, carrying a potted plant. "What are you up to?" she said suspiciously. "You look a bit puffed."

She was not to feel the least bit worried, I told her; dead plants didn't bloom in the spring, tra-la. Ridding *Kylie* of the motor only meant that I'd have to spend one or two extra days champing at the bit when passing through the Horse Latitudes. Heigh-ho, Silver! Away!

"It's leaking oil. Take it to the dump."

She must have reported the matter to Nigel, for on my light-footed return to the river he strode along the dockside and informed me I was barmy.

But there had been no two ways about it, I replied with mild heat: either the engine went out of the boat or I would take leave of my mind. The relationship between it and me had sunk to such a low ebb that it was not possible to share the same cabin with it a minute longer. Although the mechanic in the tight-fitting hat had come back from his cruise and spun spanners, the activity had not generated light. The motor had run busily but had not delivered any amps. Nor would it, the

113

workshop manual had revealed to us on pp. 62–4 when we troubled at last to open it, till a half-buried nut had been revolved with a special tool. Lockers had been rummaged and toolboxes turned out in search of the implement with which to extract the rotor but it was nowhere to be found. I wrung my hands; the mechanic tugged at the peak of his hat. Together we asked around for aid. Who in this wide dark world would bear us a spanner with the strange device?

No one within earshot on the Rio Dulce, replied boaters at an adjacent dock who spent hours networking the airwaves, nor any person in a workshop it was possible to get to by Honduran *cayuco* or Guatemalan bus. The tool would have to be flown in from Europe: four days by special delivery, huh-huh. But my model of engine and its unique spanner had gone out of production years ago, so I was in a seller's market, they went on, huh-huhing less openly. It would cost fifty dollars at least, they reckoned, plus the *mordida*.

On hearing this, the mechanic had taken his head out of his hat and left me to follow devices and desires of my own.

Though the tool was affordable, I chose not to buy it. Figures in the logbook revealed that on passages of five hundred miles or more the engine had been running one hour in every twenty-six, but on shorter journeys – such as the 200-mile passage from the Virgins to Isla Mona – it had been going for 65 per cent of the time, which suggested that, in spite of my goings-on about the joys of sailing, I had been nothing but a floating motorist. To this shaming revelation was added the depressing rider that the noise from the engine had more than likely been drowning any messages from Pip.

Knuckling his forehead, Nigel strode back to *Nada*, leaving me to scrub sump oil from my hands. In spite of the high quality of Daphne's soap my fingernails stayed edged in black.

Not far from the washplace a man with cleaner hands lay face upwards on bare boards beneath a flotilla of model boats hanging by threads below Mario's steep roof. The little wooden hulls swung to every breath of air. They moved, but they adventured nowhere; and below them his pale blue eyes stayed open.

"That fellow Jim needs to find himself a worthwhile project," said Daphne, pinching out dead flowers. Jim winced.

Pivoting a pair of sweeps about the fulcrum of the cockpit winches, I backed *Kylie* out of the marina and anchored off to wait for the wind.

To keep my word to Mrs Howell's Aunt Olive and my family I needed to sail to the Bay Islands of Honduras and from there to the east coast of the British Isles before the coming summer had ended. I polished my NHS spectacles and measured distances on a *Pilot Chart of the North Atlantic Ocean*. Allowing myself five-night stopovers the Bay Islands and Isla Mujeres and, say, ten nights each in Belize, Florida, Bermuda and the Azores amounted to 50 nights. Six thousand sea-miles would take, say, 70 days, making a grand total of 120. I could be just about entering the North Sea on 31 August.

I squeezed into the forecabin to check the lamp-locker. Decanted and filtered, the three remaining gallons of straw-coloured Mexican kerosene would be enough to brew three pints of medium-strong tea a day for each of two persons as far as Florida, as well as cook them corned-beef hashes after evening star-sights, and – except perhaps when the sea was extra lumpy – 10 fluid ounces of heavy-duty porridge.

But, I reflected while cutting out gaskets for the screw-top containers, *Kylie* is still too heavily laden. Discarding the engine, its associated bits and pieces and ten gallons of diesel fuel had lightened her by 300 lbs, but she'd sail better if even more bits and pieces were to follow the engine overboard. There were enough ancient shackles and bottlescrews in the depths of the lamp-locker to start a maritime museum. And, though feeding an extra mouth and reading its lips in all kinds weather for four months would not be the easiest of tasks, I didn't seem to have left myself much choice. The insurer had said *Kylie* must carry an extra person aboard as far as Florida, and I had told my children I would not be sailing in solitude on the Atlantic crossing. I screwed down the container tops and examined the gaskets for leaks. Head upside down within the narrow locker, bent so nearly double that my remaining acoustic nerves were for minutes rendered useless, I hoped that whoever else eventually came aboard to crew *Kylie* was in the habit of unclosing their teeth when they spoke and wore hats of a size which was compatible with their heads.

Ten feet above the Rio Dulce, securing Nigel's magnificent gift of a triple-unit solar panel which he himself had designed and fitted between the backstays, the outer corner of my left eye noticed a motorized *cayuco* careering across the river. I stared at it with a half-open mouth and an unquiet mind. Tweaking sideways at the forward-facing outboard engine propelling him backwards into the future was a tiny Indian in a vast sombrero.

From his customary platform high above, a ghostly Dimbleby took charge, slowing the onrush of events to a tolerable plod. I found myself spectating a preview of my trauma a split second before it struck me.

I knew in advance how distinctly alien my scream would sound when it came out, the size to which the Indian's eyes and mouth would open when he turned his head towards me a moment before the impact, and which parts of my stationary vehicle would disintegrate, and in what order. Though not tidings of great joy, the information was quite a help. By the time the *cayuco* actually thudded into *Kylie*'s stern and the wind-vane whirled away in the direction of a gravy-coloured pelican, I already had some inkling of how much wood and epoxy I would need for the repairs.

Two days later, watching me apply a final coat of paint to a replacement strut for the shattered wind-vane, Jim levered himself upright from Mario's floorboards and declared loudly, "I b'lieve I have a new life coming up. She's flying out to Belize ten days from now, so let's you and me sail our boats there in company, huh?"

The wind-vane was back in place at sunset. Next morning I broke to Daphne the news that Jim and I were about to leave.

"Oh, really? How absolutely wonderful to know that Jim has got himself a project at last," she replied across the counter while making out my bill.

"Well, yes, of course it is," I said. "But I get twinges of backache too, you know."

"Pull the other one," said Daphne, patting her chignon.

"Anyway, my insurer thinks I ought to get myself a partner, even if you don't."

"Does he, now? Tsk! There was a backpacker in Fronteras asking to crew, so I'll mention it to him if you want."

17

Barracuda and Baron Bliss

Simon was a tall young man from Cheshire with a high forehead and a low chuckle. Having up-ended his rucksack and shaken out what he solemnly declared was every last speck, he sat down next to his medium-size straw hat and rolled a small flimsy.

"If they find a trace anywhere, I lose the boat," I told him.

While he was lighting the cigarette I put on my glasses and confirmed that his medium-length hair was hanging from a medium-sized head.

"All right, then, we'll give it a go. I'll take you as far as the Bay Islands.

"Where'll I put these?" he said, pulling off a pair of big black boots. Judging from the absence of blisters, they too were not ill-fitting.

For the time being, they had better stay on the duckboard, I said. His smaller belongings could go into the locker above the port-side berth, where they would share space with three parachute flares, 45 disposable syringes, and a crumbling package of none-too-fragrant chemicals for the repelling of mosquitoes. He wondered aloud about the syringes.

"They're for a clinic in the Hog Islands," I told him; then, looking down at the boots, I went on: "you'd better put those in the after-midships bin, underneath the flag bag."

We weighed anchor at 9.30, waved farewell to the Calders, blew five long blasts on a conch shell and sculled into the middle of the river. Here we put up the spinnaker but the airs were so light that in two hours the boat had made only as few miles. Gurgling softly through its backside, Jim's boat glided out of Mario's and drew level.

"Tow you, huh?"

"No, thank you all the same," I said.

"See you at Cayo Grande, then."

"Of course."

"Crazy man!"

Tacking across light airs on El Golfete, in six hours *Kylie* made good the nine miles to Cayo Grande, anchoring there in four fathoms. It was good, I thought while warming up my harmonica on *Young Ladies from Bannion,* that the new crew-member's hat had stayed on his head without any help when he had rowed us back aboard in ten knots of wind after eating dinner with Jimmie.

Our two boats leapfrogged each other in soft winds down the gorge of the Rio Dulce, out on to the Bahia de Amatique and through the first of the scores of mangrove islands, palm-tree cays and sunlit reefs which cascade down the coast of the Yucatàn and Belize for 250 miles.

Hat now tied down, rod in hand, line stretched far beyond its 15-lb limit, Simon played a barracuda. We had sailed northwards from Punta Gorda in Belize against a strengthening wind and current, beating for hours outside the Snake Cays and being buffeted from time to time by squalls. After tacking, reefing, sail-changing, and drinking, between squalls, tiny tots of rum, by morning Placentia was in sight and Simon had hooked his first barracuda.

"Biggest fish I've caught in me whole life," he said, his voice throaty with awe and pride, while sprinkling cummin on to a section of its deep white flesh.

When the anchor lantern made – to my disappointment – in China had been topped up with kerosene and its wick had been pinched ready for lighting, Simon said it was about time to fetch Jim aboard to eat. His beamy vessel had motored towards us through a steep chop at noon and anchored a hundred yards away, but we had not seen him on deck since then. I rowed across and called, but no head poked out. I rapped on the hull and shouted him a second time. No one appeared.

Never known at Mario's without alcohol in his liver (but always clean shaven and very well scrubbed in spite of it), and now, lying on a marble-patterned settee in his vast cabin, great toes parallel, fingers interlocked across the chest of a long loose tunic, he looked like an early English saint. Not a bottle in sight, either; just an empty plastic beaker and a small tin of tuna. Dead to the world and a lovely fresh fish.

It was impossible to alter his attitude. I squeezed his nearest toe until his eyes opened but he wouldn't move. He wanted to get his oncoming partner between his arms, he mouthed at me, as soon as he possibly could.

"Just you take things quietly awhile!" we called to him at seven-thirty the following morning as, lurching across his foredeck in the tunic, he watched us make sail. "Follow on in an hour or so, tuck yourself in at Blue Ground Range, and tonight, I promise you, we'll cook you an absolute whopper."

Under the large genoa we beat out of Placentia, pitching to short seas on a twenty-five mile dog-leg against the current. Clear of the narrow north channel, I latched-in the wind-vane. Simon produced a second spool of line and an immense hook, which he baited with corned beef.

"What's the breaking strain of that stuff, then?"

"Three hundred pounds. We could be eating shark steak for supper, with a little bit of luck."

The wind was still at east-north-east twelve knots when Jim's boat came up staidly from astern under mainsail and engine, its mast hardly canted from the vertical and the Blue Ground Range only seven miles ahead. Above, the sky was one-eighth wispy fluff but, away to the west, a black cloud shaped like an anvil was towering above the Maya Mountains. Jim overtook us at two o'clock, when the course was 020° and the barometer stood at 990 mb. Simon had trailed his hook for two hours but had caught nothing. He wasn't to mind too much about it, I told him; bully beef was every bit as tasty as fresh shark.

Kylie chattered briefly into the eye of the wind and lay hove-to off the Blue Ground Range. We saw with dismay that Jim had anchored his boat in entirely the wrong place. His tunic lay on deck in a crumpled heap, and he was slumped over the stern rail, naked, passing water.

"Get yourself inside the lagoon. Just look at that cloud, man! If it blows up from the west you'll go aground."

"Whaddya say?" said Jim, shaking his dick.

I straddled the cockpit and cupped my hands.

"YOU ARE EXPOSED," I called sternly.

"Not half," chuckled Simon.

"Oh, for Heaven's sake shut up. He's plastered. Swim over and give him a hand to pull up his anchor and follow me in."

I beat through the western entrance into a square-mile basin of dark water girdled by sombre mangroves which would give good protection in winds from most quarters. *Kylie* anchored in forty feet, and soon afterwards Jim's bigger boat was moored safely too and he had disappeared below.

Although the anvil-shaped cloud loomed larger the weather stayed quiet. Simon swam back to *Kylie*, collected his fishing gear and rowed off to catch supper while I settled into a corner of the cockpit with my second-best pipe to enjoy the changing panorama of the sky. Before the glowing tobacco had been reduced to ashes Jims mast and rigging was crawling across the face of the sun.

"WHAT ON EARTH ARE YOU DOING?" I screamed into the walkie-talkie. Seconds later the boat ran aground.

He was able to refloat himself by going full astern with the engine, backing away into deeper water in semi-darkness. He turned in a tight circle and re-anchored. Simon tossed his rod and line into the cockpit and together we rowed in haste to aid our companion, expecting to find him in a drunken muddle, but by the time we clattered down into the cabin he had already arranged himself in a saintly position and closed his eyes. It was as though he was getting himself ready to enter the next world, said Simon with a not-very-devout gleam in his eyes as he rowed back to cook supper.

After eating it, gently pummelling cushions into a soft hummock, I thought how pleasant it was to be lying in the cabin on a calm evening, with an oil lamp gleaming and the smell of coffee prickling my nostrils; and how fortunate it had been that, in spite of the menacing thunder-cloud, the wind had never once blown hard enough to test the fit of our hats. Muttering into its skirts, the cloud had sloped off towards Guatemala, leaving us in peace.

At two o'clock in the moonless morning we were woken by Jim's fists beating on the hull. "Come on, you guys, I need help! I've been fast aground for two hours! C'mon now!"

Cursing horribly, we fought our way through the mosquito nettting into the cockpit. He had shuddered awake in panic, his head filled with the mistaken notion that his lady was about to touch down at Belize city. So pressing was his desire to hold her hand that he had straightaway pulled up the anchor and headed north out of the lagoon. How he had managed to find a way out in the darkness was a mystery. Like all the other channels in the area, the northern one was not marked by poles or withies. Half a mile into the channel, the good fortune which had accompanied him for years in California had at last deserted him, leaving him heeled over at an angle of ten degrees on a bank of hard mud.

His boat was a heavy-displacement cruiser with a long keel, a 45-horsepower engine and a windlass which was turned by electricity. If we laid out an anchor, insisted Jimmie, the windlass, goddamit, would drag her off. The claim did not seem over-bold, so Simon and I lugged out a 45-pounder and 200 lbs of chain. Jimmie thumbed a red button. As if ingesting spaghetti, the windlass sucked away busily. After several minutes of happy slurping, a series of hiccups suggested that the going was no longer good.

"Do go easy on that button," we cautioned him respectfully when the chain was taut and the boat was still not shifting, "or you'll burn out the blessed motor."

"Let me run this operation my way!" cried the overlord from his lofty castle, shutting his ears to the ghastly moans which even mine could hear were now coming from the windlass. We laid out a second anchor at a broader angle and tailed its warp to the cockpit winches, at which we wound away busily until the warp was thrumming. Then Jim in the doghouse went full ahead on the engine, at the same time bearing down on the red button. Still the boat stayed put.

"Shit!" cried Jim.

"There is no man so extreme as the disillusioned moderate," wrote John Buchan before going off to govern Canada. Now, seventy years after he wrote them, I found myself thinking his words could be true. Jim's eyes glittered, and his lips were crusted with a white rime. Even worse, he had thrown aside his hat.

The warp and chain were as stiff as rods. Simon and I toiled unprofitably at the winches.

"Come on, you guys! Put your backs into it!" came the command from on high.

We left off our labours and straightened up.

"Jimmie?" we said.

"Yes?"

"Close your mouth. The waterline is miles above the sodding water."

What steps he would have taken to put down the mutiny will never be known because at that instant the windlass sent up a small puff of white smoke.

"I believe we have a new Pope," said Simon, taking off his hat.

By this time the sun was past its best height. From the depths of nearby mangroves glided a dory bearing two solemn men in black vests and trousers. They could have been undertakers looking for custom.

"Excuse me, but when is high water?" I asked them.

"Was half an hour ago," said one, rubbing his hands.

Aloft in a bosun's chair I shackled a snatch-block to the masthead while the dory laid out a third anchor attached to a gantline which we tailed aft to a second pair of winches. All four of us cranking, slowly the boat heeled over until water was lapping the coamings and then, with its engine roaring, the dory screaming, Simon and Jim racking the windlass with an extra-long handle and me grinding my back teeth, twelve hours after it had run onto the bank the heavy hull slithered sideways and lurched upright.

The men climbed aboard from the dory and sat in the shade of the bimini, clutching beers. Jimmie and I sprawled on the coachroof, gasping like landed fish. Simon rolled himself a flimsy and asked the men what the best bait was, and soon afterwards he rowed off to catch our supper, leaving Jimmie and me to re-anchor the boat once more in the lagoon.

By this time it was too late in the day to make for the next anchorage. And, surely, I remarked to Simon later while watching him prepare a red snapper for the pan, *surely* by this time even a go-getter from California wouldn't try to lift his colossal anchor by hand and run his bloody great boat aground on a bloody great shoal yet again . . .

"I wouldn't bet on it," said Simon.

He was right. Before long a familiar mast and rigging had crawled across the face of the sun and had got itself stuck fast in the very same place.

Simon looked at me; I looked at him. Both of us contemplated the red snapper. Before rowing over to help, we ate it.

Two days later *Kylie* came abreast of Belize city in a stiff breeze, bringing up into the wind near the curiously-named Baron Bliss lighthouse in eight feet of water. Rowing *Kylie*'s dinghy any distance across the current would be asking for a dousing, so we had anchored as near to the Fort George jetty as was possible. Between *Kylie* and the shore, and only fifty yards off the jetty, in what I knew from an earlier visit was no more than five feet of water, was an elderly New Yorker in an ancient sloop.

In the shelter of *Kylie*'s cockpit I poured kerosene into the anchor lantern and cleaned the day's dottle from my pipe. On the foredeck of the sloop a frail white-haired figure took down a pair of flapping trousers from the rigging, shuffled aft along the sidedeck and carried them below. To murmurs of deep appreciation from us, Jimmie anchored his boat half a mile to the south-east in twelve feet of water, well clear of shoals and banks. It seemed possible that we might have a good night's sleep.

By the time Baron Bliss was flashing a red light once every five seconds Jim's dinghy was bounding past us through sheets of spray, past the ancient sloop and onwards to the Fort George Hotel. He had invited us to go ashore with him but, good companion though he always was, it was not difficult to find sound reasons for staying aboard *Kylie*: letters needed to be written home; Simon wanted to listen to the BBC World Service; we felt altogether done in. I hung the anchor light in the rigging, Simon put headphones on, and soon we were sinking into sleep.

But not for long. At midnight there came again the dreadful thuds on the hull.

"I don't believe this. What's up now?"

"Boat's aground!"

"Piss off."

"Listen! The old man from New York is hard aground . . .! An' he's so sick that he might die tomorrow, just like the guy who set me on my way to California and then dropped dead!" Jimmie was lunging at us through the guardrails, beating on the coachroof, sobbing. "And now – goddammit . . . all the pile I've made! – don' you *see*? – it isn't *mine*! I owe this old man all I've got . . .! *Move*, you guys! We got to save him!"

He bullied us into his dinghy and we bounded off on our mission of mercy.

"What's the matter with it?" I screamed above the snarling engine. The sloop's mast was upright and its anchor warp was leading off fairly from the bows. "It looks all right to me."

I spoke too soon. In the beam of the flashlight we saw the sloop was pinned by wind and current on to the shoal. We jostled alongside and were instantly entangled in frayed rope-ends and plastic buckets.

"You're aground!" cried Jimmie, thwacking flakes of paint off the hull as Simon shone the beam on the tell-tale fringe of glistening weed an inch or so above the present waterline,

Above a buckled guardrail appeared a large white head. It looked like that of Albert Einstein.

"Something bothering you?" enquired the head, its hair dancing to the wind.

"You're hard aground!"

"Yes, yes!" it cried with glee. "I know I am! But it doesn't bug me one bit! Y'see, I like it here."

Its large eyes peered at us keenly through the torchlight. Just from glimpsing them, you felt that they knew what you were going to say before you so much as opened your mouth. It was difficult to believe, however, that they were entirely sane.

"Hard right rudder!"

"I don't think you . . ."

"Hard right!"

"But, boys, I . . ."

"Fire the motor! Full forward and hard right! Lay out another anchor!"

The figure in the cockpit gave a shrug. "Well, okay . . . If it will make you feel any happier, just you go right ahead and do what you want . . ."

We clambered aboard and bustled about our salvage drill. Calling briskly to one other across the swirling current, soon we had laid out a second anchor and were heaving away in unison on the foredeck.

"Hoolah-tie!"

"Hah!"

"Mealey-my!"

"Hoh!"

" . . .Doyle for his boots!"

We hung over the rail and stared into the water. Below us swam reflections of Baron Bliss's red eye. Simon spat at them.

"Heck! We gotta get him off," gasped Jimmie, wiping his nose with the back of his left hand and his eyes with the back of his right. "Let's take a line to the masthead and haul him off. C'mon, you guys: up the mast!"

"Hang on . . .," said Simon, clearing his throat. "Where the devil has he got to?"

We cleated the lines and went in search. The wheel had been clamped hard a-starboard and the motor was running at three-quarters throttle, but the cockpit had nobody in it.

We opened the hatch.

The old man was lying in his berth, leafing through a comic.

18

You and I

After a 19-day passage through boisterous weather, John L Stephens, an earlier visitor from New York who was also thought to be in frail health, was met on landing near that same mudbank off Belize city by a gentleman named Coffin. In spite of this none-too-encouraging augury, the American then rode hundreds of miles on horseback, over roads so atrociously bad that at the end of one twelve-hour stint in the saddle he had covered only ten miles. When at last the going became too difficult for horses, Stephens hacked his way through dense jungle infested with malarial mosquitoes and eventually came upon a lost Mayan city, which he bought for $50 (£31.25).

On learning of this historic transaction, Simon concealed a £5 ($8) note in his boots and clumped off towards the nearest forest. While he was absent Jimmie and I sailed our boats to a mosquito-free marina which had been dug out of the sandy island of Cay Chapel. From this pleasant haven he whirred away to Belize city in a water-taxi to seek out his helpmate in life's struggle while I went off sailing in *You and I*.

Months ago this boat had been one of a small flotilla which had sailed through our anchorage off Ambergris Cay in twenty knots of wind. My cry that the boats were coming had brought Nigel on deck with his camera and we had then watched a sight impossible to forget. In all the years of *Kylie*'s travels there have been scores of days which have been very much alike, but this day at Ambergris was to be unique, for never till then had I seen a group of laden cargo-boats at speed under sail.

Their stems raked forward to short bowsprits and their hulls were a melody of curves. I had seen many daintier hulls, and sails which set better on their spars, and none of these boats would have won a prize for the quality of its fittings or standard of maintenance. The cumbrous anchors were thick with rust and the eyes in the galvanised wire rigging had been more often closed with bulldog grips than with splices, and yet that afternoon the Calders and I did not look admiringly at any other boats but these. In the brittle sunlight we had watched their bow waves curl above a seabed of coral sand which was strewn here and there with dark green eel-grass. Going at her fastest but hardly heeling, *You and I* had surged past with one man at the weather shrouds and another at the tiller until, half a mile beyond our anchorage, the figure had moved from the shrouds to the mast, the mainsail had flapped briefly, an anchor had been cast over the bows and the boat had been eased back on to a quay and its crew had set about unloading.

Apart from their comeliness, what had kept my eyes fixed on these boats was that, unlike any other fleet of sail I had ever seen, all of them were carrying cargoes for profit, engaged in the line of work which my Liverpool grandfather had followed when he had owned sailing-barges on the Mersey. It was a way of life which my mother had seen for a few years as a girl until the steam engine had put paid to sail but, although she had told me of these times, until now I myself had not seen sail-traders going about about their business.

But now, aboard *You and I*, for a few hours I could be part of it.

Though she had been built in Belize to carry cargoes through the hazards of the coral reef, across warm shallow sand-bars and up jungly rivers where the breeze was shut out by tropical trees, *You and I* would have equally well suited the estuaries of Suffolk and Essex. Thirty-two feet from stem to stern, with a $9^1/_2$-foot beam and a laden draught of five feet, she carried a sliding gunter gaff – called locally an antenna – on a mast stepped well forward of the centre. To this antenna was laced the upper forward edge of a huge mainsail, the foot of which was roped to a bamboo boom 25 feet long. In the early fifties as many as a hundred of these swift and sturdy craft had been plying the inshore waters of the Gulf of Honduras but now, forty years on, there were no more than three dozen of them still working.

Among them *You and I* was by no means the least, nor were the men who worked her. In the space of ten hours Howard Arnold and Edward Flores had shovelled seven tons of sand from the seabed, pitching it up over their shoulders into the hull, sailed it 20 miles from Cay Chapel to Ambergris and shovelled it out again on to the quayside, and now they were sailing home with their wages. In all, this amounted to 75 Belizean dollars (US $37.50 or £23.44), to be divided out three ways.

"Twenty-five dollars for the owner and the rest is for us," said Howard, "but sometimes, when we carry things like fridges and furniture, we can make 400." (US $200 or £125).

126

In light winds we sailed towards their home at Mullins River, following the white ribbon of channel through Porto Stuck. Across the width of the hull Edward dragged a three-foot metal bowl half-filled with sand, criss-crossed kindling wood at its centre and lit a fire, above which he stood a billycan of fish stew. Behind him at the stern, with the unpainted tiller lodged comfortably in his armpit, squatted Howard.

And as they sailed homeward with their wages, in a hull with scarred and pitted planking, beneath rusting wire rigging set up on wooden deadeyes and rope lanyards, I told them that their stew tasted very good.

You and I.

19

Cay Caulker

"There's loads more to come," whispered the blonde.

She was filling my arms with bottles she had taken from the settee onto which Jim, minutes earlier, had sunk. In the two hours since they had taxied back hand-in-hand to Cay Chapel, she seemed to have found her feet and much else.

"Honey, I do believe it's time for you to go," were the next words spoken by the handmaiden while passing down the overlord's last remaining quart of vodka. The invitation to leave was half-expected. From hints which had passed between them before Jim had crawled to his couch, I had become aware of this drastic plan to save his liver. As so often happens when called upon to save people from their excesses, I was in at least two minds about its merits, a pert voice from my mother's side arguing that abstinence makes the heart grow fonder; another, in a tone tinged with vinegar, declaring the only way to a man's heart was through his stomach; and a third asking wryly why the target of love's arrows was always so bally close to a man's wallet.

My role as an accomplice was made no easier by these murmurs from the past. Like a not-very-witting pirate in a comic opera, I leered gamely into the eyes of the all-conquering nursemaid, raised a sail to the afternoon breeze and made off into a passing rain cloud with the plunder.

I went only three miles, to just as far as Cay Caulker. As well as being a likely market for *Kylie*'s unwanted gear, Cay Caulker is the island where fishing-smacks like *You and I* had first appeared in Belize and where the latest hull was being planked, so I had been told, by a man named Nelson. Until I talked to Howard and Edward in *You and I*, I had had the feeling that the smacks were based on a design brought out in the 1850s from, probably, Essex by a migrant forester who had later grown weary of cutting mahogany and taken up inshore fishing. In fact, the first of the smacks had not been built until 1911, and then for a Señor Belisario Rodriguez, a resident of Cay Caulker, to a design which had been imported from no farther than Cuba. Among the novel attractions of the design in Belizean eyes were two watertight bulkheads forming a well in which the catch was kept alive by seawater flowing in and out through holes bored in the hull. To me, though, not the least interesting thing about the vessel was its name. What kind of a name would a man with the name of Rodriguez be expected to give to a beautifully swift boat of Hispano-American stock? Something

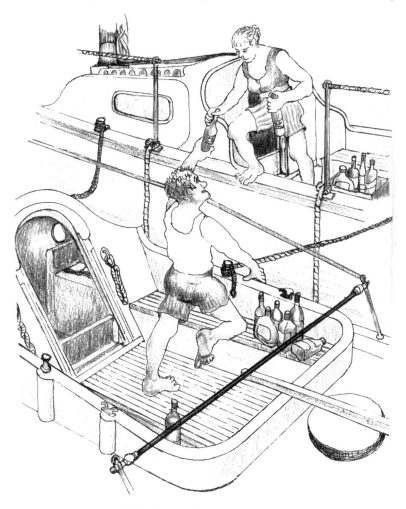

"There's loads more to come"

sprightly and Spanish, such as *Golondrina,* a swallow? But he didn't. This was happening in 1911, when the British Empire was still near its peak, so Belisario Rodriguez had called the boat *Lion.*

On rowing ashore in the evening to offer items of boat-gear for sale, I tied *Kylie*'s dinghy to a jetty at which lay what seemed to be another of these handsome craft. Although it was about the same length as *You and I,* from what I could see of it in the weak lighting it was in other ways quite different. *You and I* had been virtually an open boat, with only a short foredeck and a small lazarette at the stern, but this boat was almost fully decked, its sheerline rose to a taller bow, the mast raked sharply and, instead of ending in a bluff stern, its hull tapered to a slightly raked sternpost on which hung a slender rudder with a steering yoke.

I peered at the bows. Was there a cranze iron at the waterline to take a bobstay, as on *You and I?* I knelt to examine the stem more closely. In black lettering below its rubbing-strake was the name *Lion.* I was looking at the first Belizean smack boat, eighty years old and still in service. And, as I knelt there gazing at its hull, I believe that I heard a child singing *Where have all the flowers gone?* I lit an ancient briar pipe. As the first smoke rose from its bowl the small voice fell silent. Even so, it seemed to me at that moment that so long as the names *Lion* and Nelson were on people's lips the old Empire would not have quite passed away.

From two smiling islanders on the jetty I learned that *Lion*'s hull-planking of Douglas fir and its ribs of cypress were the originals, and that a modern version of the design was being built by Nelson Young only a couple of hundred paces down the road.

What comes first, cash or contemplation? I carried my bits and pieces of gear southward along the sandy track to Center's Bar, where I sought out a troubled Irishman who had been gripped by a sudden urge to write a novel.

"Why not get cracking, then? Strike while the iron's hot."

"Can't," he said glumly. "I have no typewriter."

"Could you make use of this one ?" I said, holding up an Empire-made model of the 1960s, which in minutes I had sold to him for more than it had cost me.

Put into good spirits by this, I bought half a gallon of carbonated water to mix with Jim's vodka.

"You lookin' for Nelson?" cried an aged crone in a dusty bandanna next morning when at last I rinsed my face and went in search of him.

She was sweeping sand from her yard before the afternoon wind drifted it back again. Behind, tilted on to its bilge, lay the hull of Nelson's boat. It carried the same lines as *You and I* but, like *Lion*, it was fully decked and had coamings fitted into place for a cabin.

The woman laid a scrawny forearm on the top of the broom handle and screeched "Nelson!"

A shed door swung open and there emerged a small wiry man wearing large dark spectacles. He lit a cigarette and was instantly racked by a bout of coughing.

"The planking is Santa Maria," he replied huskily to my questions, "but the ribs are cypress, same as *Lion*."

"So will you rake her mast like *Lion*?"

"Argh! (Cough, cough) No!"

"What about its sails?" I went on shamelessly, for he really did sound groggy. He rubbed at his throat with bent fingers and croaked that the rig would be very like the one carried by *You and I*. It was the information for which I had been fishing.

"Well, now! I happen to have a foresail which might suit you," I said, trying to appear calmer than I felt.

He looked at me with sudden interest, and soon his gnarled fingers were stroking *Kylie*'s old No. 2 genoa, which had cost me £90 ($144) new in 1978.

"Yes, oh ye-e-e-ss . . .," he crooned between coughs and rattles; "the sailcloth is wery *good*."

Leaving him to stroke it, I hurried back to Center's Bar to keep an appointment with a man from San Francisco, to whom I sold three ancient but sturdy bottlescrews, and to show another sail to an island fisherman. The bottlescrews went quite quickly but selling the sail took a couple of hours. From time to time during the negotiations I caught glimpses of Nelson. Once, he was standing on a fretworked verandah, waving a machete at a scowling man who was handing him dollar notes. Nelson, it seemed to me, was not so much brandishing the machete as holding it up for inspection, and so I supposed that the shipwright was also the island's knife-grinder and that I was witnessing the closing stages of a business deal between Nelson and a not-very-satisfied customer. The next time I saw him he was hunched beneath a palm tree near the police station and an officer was shouting rebukes onto his bowed and grizzled head. Having myself been bundled by this same officer into the police station at midnight in the baseless hope that my pipe was filled with cannabis, I knew he was not the friendliest of bobbies.

With the briar pipe in my deepest pocket, I hurried past this depressing cameo until I got into the shade of a bushy tree. I squatted down to count the takings.

Nelson limped into the shade, shorter of breath than ever after being talked to by the local police force.

"Will you . . . aah . . . take . . . aargh . . . a hundred and seventy for that sail?"

"What's that you said?" I said, cupping an ear towards him and frowning.

"Two hundred, then? You *got* to take two hundred!" He was racked by another spasm of coughing. Sweat glistened on his cheekbones. "I can't get no more than two hundred . . ."

"All right, Nelson, I'll take your two hundred."

He went off, his left foot dragging in the sand. I folded his banknotes into my wad and began to reckon up how much profit had been made.

The total arrived at in *Kylie*'s cabin shocked me: the day's takings, 550 Belizean dollars ($275 or £171.86), would have been thought a modest enough week's wages in England, but here in Cay Caulker they were as much as Howard, Edward or Nelson might very well earn in a month. More to the point, ten per cent of it was profit. I poured carbonated water into two fingers of Jim's vodka and leafed through a glossy mail-order catalogue.

Boots hanging round his neck, hot but happy from his foray into the jungle, Simon water-taxied back to *Kylie*. He dumped the rucksack on the foredeck, peeled off his tee-shirt and plunged over the side. I sippped carbonated vodka and wrote out an order for a pair of state-of-the-art binoculars. Before I could put it in an envelope Simon was swimming at speed back to *Kylie*.

"Where's the snorkel? There's a family of dolphins in the bay. I'm going to stroke them."

I rowed ashore to fax off the binocular order before the office closed. It was almost dark, and *Lion* lay at the dock in the gloaming. Nelson Young, grandson of the shipwright who had built her, shuffled out of the bushes at the head of the jetty and stood before me. His left shoulder, I noticed, was a good two inches higher than his right.

"You leaving tomorrow?"

"Perhaps," I said warily.

"Please take this," he said, pressing a smooth piece of wood into my palm.

132

"No, really, Nelson; I can't."

"Take it, man!" cried Nelson. "You are my very good friend from England who has let me have a sail for my boat!"

"Heck, I didn't *give* you it!" I called after him as he limped off through the bushes.

In my hand lay a half-model of a smack hull. I rowed back to *Kylie* and switched on the brightest light. Seven layers of Santa Maria had been glued to form a block which had then been pared and sanded into a harmony of curves. Made to a scale of half an inch to the foot, it was neither a toy nor an ornament but a shipwright's working model. From it, offsets would be drawn onto baulks of cypress which would be sawn into full-size ribs. The model had not been made on purpose to delight my eye but so that men with gnarled hands might eke out a living from the sea. It was priceless.

Minutes later, Simon was telling me about his swim and I was cooking supper.

"The dolphins were unbelievably trustful. 'Course, the mother was nervous on account of the young one, but she let me stroke her. And . . ., you know . . ., *she talked*! She was making little squeaks, telling me to please not go too close to her baby. God, it was wonderful! It was like . . . it was like . . .!" He raised his hands and touched his forehead. His eyes glinted.

"Golly! Really?"

I set up the table, turned up the oil lamp and served out spaghetti bolognaise.

I began telling him of how I had sold profitably the sails and other unwanted items, not only to visitors from the USA and Europe but to the island people too.

"Really?" said Simon. "That a fact?"

Before I came to the end of my account he got up from the table, pulled aside the mosquito net and went up into the cockpit.

"Where you going? Don't you want any afters?"

"No, thanks. I'd rather like to listen to that dolphin again."

And *Kylie* heeled away from me as he dived in.

20
Hold-up on Albert Street

On a tepid grey morning at Cay Caulker the wind backed sixty degrees and blew from the Yucatán, dragging thin ragged clouds across a sky the colour of our watery porridge. I put *Kylie*'s papers and our passports into a rucksack, along with Nigel's sketch-plan of Belize city, telling Simon as I did so that we ought to clear out from the city for the Bay Islands that same morning, before the north wind veered east again. Under a red-and-green spinnaker, *Kylie* surged along the sandy channel through Porto Stuck, and at eleven anchored in a stiff breeze off Baron Bliss light, fifty yards downwind of the ancient sloop on which Einstein was again taking down flapping trousers from the rigging.

"What do I do if the old boy drags his anchor and drifts down on me?" called Simon with a rare hint of anxiety before I rowed away in the dinghy.

"For a start, you could ask him to lend you his favourite comic. If that doesn't scare him off, I'm afraid that you'll just have to pay out more rope."

Walking is an activity about which I seldom turn lyrical, and from Nigel's sketch it looked as if the coming footslog to the Customs, Immigration and Harbour authorities would be long and tedious, for two of those grand officials held court in well-separated blocks of the city centre, while the office of the third and greatest grandee lay a mile or so outside it. In spite of the need to clear out quickly I stopped on the swing bridge which spans Haulover Creek so as to look closely at a line of smacks moored in midstream. A shopper with a bagful of groceries brushed past me on the narrow footpath. On the foredeck of the nearest boat a woman soaped an infant, ladling water onto its head while another child stood by at the ready with a towel. Though the sight of this delightful family idyll detained me only seconds, it gave enough time to a bare-headed man in jungle-camouflage clothing to shamble through a crawl of cars in Albert Street and position himself squarely in front of me the moment I stepped off the bridge. The whites of his bulging eyes were laced red and tight crinkles of black hair above his forehead had bits of straw in them. He glared into my face and scowled horribly.

"Money!"

"Do speak up," I said, unwilling to credit what had come from his lips.

"Ten fucking dollars!"

"No."

He made indelicate motions with his hands.

"Get lost."

"Then Ah'm gonna fucking stick you!" he cried, thrusting a hand into a jacket pocket where, I supposed, he kept his knife. A woman squeezed past us, carrying a melon on her shoulder. Though I was keeping my eyes fixed on my attacker's twisted lips, they could not help noticing the multitude of straight-faced Belizeans in plain-coloured shirts with nothing more deadly than ballpoints in their pockets who pressed past on either side, only inches from this arresting melodrama. None of them was caring a hoot.

The man waggled his knife-pocket in the direction of my stomach.

"Ten dollars!"

"Go away!"

At this he lifted his hands to his head and staggered sideways. His clenched fists beat at his own temples. Untroubled, passers-by swirled round him and, without a glance, pressed on. The man swayed into the traffic on Albert Street. A car hooted, a door slammed, and a soft-footed policeman brought a hand down on his shoulder and led him away into a side-street, gibbering.

Not long after this unhappy encounter Belize Customs were confronted by an agitated Englishman whose none-too-stiff upper lip must have made it hard for them to suppress a smile, but they listened to him quite gravely.

"Really, sir," they said when he had ended his tale, "there's no need for you to go all the way to the Port Captain; his office is miles away."

"But . . . er . . . what about your Defence Regulations?" I asked in low tones, for in the past weeks the smouldering border-dispute with Guatemala had shown signs of bursting into flame; our side had sent a battalion of Gurkhas to the frontier and it had been said at Mario's that the coastal waters were being patrolled by armed launches. Knowing this, I was not too keen to be caught among the cays without a proper chitty.

"Don't you worry, sir; I'll tell him that I've cleared you."

"But . . .?"

"Something else?"

"Would you mind putting that in writing?"

The hold-up.

21

Meeting a Survivor

Buffeted by the Norther, I rowed back to *Kylie* through short steep waves.

"'E equals 'em seas squared," remarked Simon as we lashed down the dinghy under the gaze of the aged Einstein who was beaming at us from his windswept cockpit.

Using the reefed mainsail and small jib, we broke out the anchor from its bed of mud and sailed briskly into the lee of the North Drowned Cays, where we lost no time in letting go of it again, because by then the day was too far gone for us to get clear of the offlying Turneffe Island before nightfall. The island lies on a broad shallow plateau five to fifteen miles east of the main barrier reef and is made up of scores of low islets covered in dismal mangroves. Cay Bokel, the southernmost, was a four-hour sail from the North Drowned Cays, and although Coxen's Hole in the Bay Islands lay a hundred miles beyond it, we stood a good chance of arriving there in less than twenty-four hours if we set off while the north wind held.

Beneath a leaden sky which pelted us from time to time with rain, next morning Simon heaved up the anchor again and bowsed it down on its chocks. Soon *Kylie* was scudding southwards at six knots down the main sugar-boat channel and I was stirring a mugful of tea.

"Why d'you go on doing it?" enquired Simon.

"Doing what?"

"Putting sugar in. 'White Death' I call it. It furs up your arteries no end."

Not the smallest difficulty of growing old is that of keeping a straight face when being taken to task by the young.

"You're right, I suppose. Sugar may do me in, but there could be worse fates."

"Such as . . .?"

"Don't know. Driving round the North Circular Road . . .? Being mail-shot by *Reader's Digest* . . .? Haven't thought about it," I said.

This last statement, however, was a lie.

"Drowning?"

"Shouldn't think so. Nearly drowned off Majorca, once. At the time it seemed like a pleasant way to go, not painful at all. Hypothermia made me nicely drowsy and then I found myself sitting down to drink tea with half a dozen gorgeous princesses. 'One lump or two?' said one as her companions were wringing out my underpants."

"You're making it up! WHAT HAPPENED NEXT . . .?"

"It's true. I behaved rather too affectionately towards them and was bundled off to jail by the police. I think they mistook me for a secret agent who was stalking a visiting queen."

Simon buckled on a safety harness as English Cay light on the barrier reef drew abeam at the start of his first sea-passage under sail. Now the water was suddenly twelve hundred feet deep, and the wind, which for hours had been blowing strongly from the north-west, swung to the north. He paid out the logline over the stern and set the dial hands at zero while I rove a preventer guy on the main boom. For the first time in months *Kylie* began to pitch and roll to deepwater swells. The lift and scend of the hull excited me. Shedding the engine and other metalwork had given extra liveliness to her motion. She was rising to the seas earlier and sliding back in the troughs hardly at all, and there was no doubt in my mind that she was going faster. I hummed *Rolling Home to Rio* and gazed ahead above the waves, but in the course of a series of watery surges during the third and fifth stanzas it occurred to me that my attitude to *Kylie* might be biased. I sought the views of the impartial witness huddled in a corner of the cockpit.

"She's going well, don't you think?"

"No!" This from a cowled head.

"Oh, come *on*!" I shone the flashlight on the whirring log. "Twenty-five miles in four hours . . .?"

"Grr!"

I lifted a corner of the hood and peered within. "You look like a Capuchin. Are you all right?"

The words of his reply were lost amid the crash of a breaker on the hull but the tone in which he spoke them suggested that Simon was feeling a good deal less lively than he would have liked. His sufferings stopped for a while at about midnight when the wind fell light and the motion became gentler, but by six in the morning it was blowing at twenty-five knots again, the companionway was shuttered and his face was once more white and waxy.

The grey hummocks of Roatan appeared above the horizon at the time of morning at which, not so long ago on the green and level plain of Cheshire, he would have been tucking in to a three-course breakfast. I told him that in four hours at the most his ordeal would be over, and I thought at the time that I was only stating the obvious. *Kylie* was then under a small jib and double-reefed mainsail, beam-on to a north-north-easterly wind, skittering through moderate-to-heavy seas and swells, sails drenched with spray, making more than six knots towards the western point of an island which lay dead ahead and only eighteen miles distant. What prospect of bliss could be plainer? In three hours we should be off the headland, and in another should have covered the remaining few miles into Coxen's Hole, still with enough of the morning left for Simon to unravel his intestines and fill them with syruped pancakes.

The prediction went badly wrong. Not for the first time when a haven was drawing near, I had fallen into the trap of thinking the wind we were presently getting would stay with us long enough to get into port. Only two miles short of the headland it was still strong from NNE, so it seemed certain we would be anchored in Coxen's Hole by eleven at the latest. But even before the boat had drawn into the lee of the land the wind fell away and the waves became floppy. Reefs were shaken out and larger foresails set, but *Kylie*'s speed through the water fell from six knots to less than three. In the space of two hours we changed headsails three times and tacked five times while the wind swung back and forth through eight compass-points. By the middle of the afternoon the log was recording two and a half knots through the water but we were being pushed backwards over the seabed by a diabolic current which was causing Coxen's Hole to grow smaller by the minute.

"Ruffles on the water to starboard . . . Let's edge over that way a bit . . ."

As *Kylie* slid towards them they vanished.

Eight hours after rounding the headland *Kylie* at last crept into harbour, by which time it was utterly dark and we were frowning deeply. It had taken from eleven in the morning till seven at night to gain five miles. To add to the enchantment, my favourite pipe disappeared overboard in the act of anchoring and we were set upon by hordes of mosquitoes.

We took cover behind screens in the cabin.

"What an awful hole Coxen's Hole is! Are the insects here always as bad as this?" Simon asked, scratching at his ankles.

"Too right! We must get out very early tomorrow."

"Why's that?"

"When daylight comes the no-see-ums take over and their bites are worse."

We didn't leave Coxen's Hole on that day or the one after it however, because the Norther blew at gale force. Other boats sought refuge and anchored too near us, so that *Kylie* became short of swinging-room. I hung a weight on the cable and glowered heavily at the port captain's office, working up a lather at the thought of the *mordida* he was going to filch from my pocket.

To my surprise he charged me only a third of what I had expected; it seemed that Nigel's thunderous protest to the Honduran government had landed on the right desk. With a pacified mind and attended by only a few listless midges, most of whose companions seemed to have been whisked to kingdom come by the gale, we beat eastward up the coast in search of more swinging-room, and in two hours were reaching north-westward up a narrow channel between reefs into Brick Bay. Here, in the lee of a small cay we anchored in thirty feet of water, astern of the only other vessel in sight, a sumptuous ketch named *Gulliver*. After the cramped anchorage at Coxen's Hole, conditions now seemed almost perfect. The gale had blown itself out, and *Kylie*'s bows were nuzzling into a pleasant breeze which, whether angled into the cabin by the windscoop or blowing directly along the coachroof under the awning, was cooling us most agreeably. I smoked a pipe; Simon munched ginger biscuits. We regretted that we had run out of beer.

As though responding to this thought, a dinghy whirred out from *Gulliver* carrying six cans of lager.

"I'm John Campbell," said its smiling, stocky driver.

"Good Lord! This is amazing."

I meant it. Seventeen years previously John Campbell had been alone aboard *Kylie* when she had been overtaken by a great Atlantic storm 400 miles west of the Azores. During the night before the storm had reached its height, when the gale had seemed to be nothing very much out of the ordinary, he had taken in all sail and let *Kylie* lie to the weather while he went below to rest. For hours she had ridden the waves sturdily, but at nine in the morning had been rolled over sideways by a large breaker. When *Kylie* had levered herself back to near-vertical, John had struggled from the flooded cabin into the cockpit. By then the wind was hurricane force, with gusts of 90 knots being reported by a nearby ship. John had steered his waterlogged boat downwind through mountainous seas and had managed to pump out most of the water, but an hour or so later *Kylie* was again overwhelmed, this time by a wave the size of an office block. And this time, instead of rolling over sideways, *Kylie* had been pitchpoled end-over-end.

The human mind quite likes to be fed tasty morsels of horror now and then, and so it is not entirely unappealing to picture the plight of a helpless human being in a small boat hurtling head-over-heels down a cliff, but the mind finds it rather less easy to accept that such a boat and its occupant could come through the experience altogether intact. I therefore greeted John Campbell with more than usual curiosity.

"Amazing . . .," I said again, and straightaway felt slightly fooolish, for the temperature of the hand which I was shaking felt no different from my own.

But what, after all, does one say in greeting a stranger whose home one has acquired? Not just his living-place, but his fixtures and fittings, his bunk-beds, mattresses, curtains, pots, pans, clock, and personal mementoes? And, more than that, what could I say to someone who had survived a hurricane in it? By comparison, the knockdown I had suffered in *Kylie* in the North Sea seemed trivial: falling sideways off a twenty-foot wave was one thing, but cartwheeling down the front of a sixty-footer was quite another.

"*Do* come aboard," I said.

John Campbell sat in the cockpit, one hand holding a can of lager, the other resting lightly on the mainsheet horse. He had written that his last act before *Kylie* pitchpoled had been to cling to the horse, a horizontal steel tube at the rear of the cockpit. What must the man be thinking as he held it again, seventeen years later? I wanted to ask him if he would have done differently: whether he thought that lying a-hull to a gale was less dangerous than running before it, and whether, in *Gulliver*, he now treated all oncoming bad weather as though it contained a potential hurricane, even when – as when he had been in *Kylie* – it came upon him outside the hurricane season. The questions were impossible for me to put to him then, though, knowing him better now, I am sure that he would have answered them directly.

"So you'll be heading back across very soon?" he said, after a while.

"I thought to leave Bermuda in early June, make the Azores in July and Ireland in August."

He crumpled up the lager can and smiled. "Well, you must call in for a drink of some stronger stuff than this when you get there," he said; "I've got a house in County Cork."

Made a little light-headed by these words, I said that I would.

141

22

Simon Goes to Paradise

The thought of meeting John in Ireland with a pint of Guinness at my elbow gave a fillip to my preparations for the Atlantic passage. High on the jobs list was the item "Check rigging", with a large red asterisk next to it. Although the starting date of the hurricane season was a couple of months in the future, for weeks I had been peering at the mast and shrouds through a magnifying glass, searching for cracks in the swages and fittings. "If you look after the boat, the boat will look after you," had said the lamp-trimmer from Aberdeen while splicing the rigging of a ship which, weeks later, emerged from a cyclone with its spars still in their appointed places. In spite of the fact that the sayings of this wise old seaman had always sustained me, thinking about what might happen if *Kylie* met with a wave the size of John Campbell's was making me feel weak at the knees.* This infirmity was one more reason why I had to make sure that *Kylie*'s mast stayed always at the right and proper angle to her body. With boats, correct deportment is everything. A man's limbs might fold up, but his boat's mustn't.

The next item read "Paint bottom". While getting ready for this tedious task I fell foul of a devious mechanic.

"It's too damn high," he said. He had driven a truck at breakneck speed along the dusty road from French Harbour with instructions to haul my boat out of the water but was now staring aloft with both hands in his pockets. Above a shirt patterned with images of sunflowers, his face wore the wintry look of a man who always knows too well what is what.

"It's not," I said.

"What's yer draft?"

"Four feet," I told him, crossing my fingers. In all, thirty-two feet eight inches of hull and mast lay between *Kylie*'s waterline and the top

---

* A pundit who spent his days among figures put the chances of meeting a wave of this height at 600,000 to 1.

of the tricolour lantern at which he was staring. Getting rid of the engine and the bottlescrews had reduced the draft by about an inch, but she was still floating deeper than her designer had intended.

"No can do." He pointed to a power cable which hung above the slipway. "Your mast won't go under it."

It crossed my mind that I was in grave danger of being diddled. I had spent two hours cultivating the owner of a waterside hotel in the hope of getting him to haul my boat up his slipway. He was an energetic Italian, eager to add to his clientele now that the island's airport was receiving international flights, but not at all sure about the English he had used in the first draft of his new brochure. He asked me what I thought of it. I replied that the meaning was clear enough but in places the expression was a little stilted. Then, for the first time in my life, I tried to barter words for deeds. Would he, I asked, after throwing a stick into the water for his golden retriever, haul out my boat if I re-wrote his brochure? It depended on the quality of the finished product, he said with a canny smile. To the dismay of the dog, I then disappeared indoors. The re-draft had so delighted the Italian that he had said I could use his slipway free of charge. His promise had given me much pleasure. Three pages of handwriting in exchange for the hauling-out of three tons of boat had seemed fair. But now a hireling in a flowery shirt seemed to be doing his best to sabotage the deal.

I measured the distance between the surface of the slipway and the bearing faces of the haulout cradle.

"If I take the lamp off the top I'm sure she'd scrape under."

"No way," he said, and sauntered back to his truck.

Into this impasse roared a taxi bearing Laurence Clegg. Spruce, resourceful, oceanic sailor, friend of the oppressed, he had flown out to sail with me as far as Florida.

"What's the matter?"

By this time I was reeling with frustration.

"That man over there says *Kylie* can't get under that wire."

The jet-lagged chum of the downcast took six paces backwards and squinted upwards. "He's right, you know; the mast's too tall."

At that moment I could have kicked him.

" 'Course it is," came a voice from the truck. "I just told him that."

Simon loped along the dockside with the morning's catch. He halted some yards off and raised an eyebrow.

"All right," I said, "time for you to have a go. Will she or won't she? What do you think?"

143

Simon put down the fish, slid a cigarette paper between his lips and walked closer.

"I think that the gentleman in the truck is looking for ten dollars," he murmured.

"I hadn't thought of that. Go and speak to him at once."

Within the hour *Kylie* had been winched out of the water and I was prising the lid off a tin of anti-fouling paint.

Into a twenty-knot breeze three men in a newly-painted boat beat out from Roatan towards the Hog Islands, twenty miles to the south. At the end of a four-hour passage they luffed into sharp flurries in the lee of the Lion's Head and sailed into the bay of Cochino Grande, where they moored to a white plastic buoy near the small meadow in which the palomino was munching its dinner. Here, as the sun moved down towards the skyline of trees above Pelican Point they dived into deep clear water and swam about the boat among small brisk waves. Here, they pegged damp towels to the guardrail and drank warm lager in the cockpit, and here, when the silver-and-green leaves in the west turned dark olive, they steamed fish.

The ridged headland on a nearby island which had been brown, orange and puce in the afternoon sunshine was now shadowed mauve and grey.

"It says 'Bonkes Nose' on the map. That must be a mistake. Who'd ever have a name like 'Bonk' . . .?"

"Lovely, this. Not many bones, either . . ."

"Is that the one they call Paradise?"

"No, it's a mile or two over there."

"I can't see it – too dark."

"Turn up the wick a bit; I've come across some bones . . ."

Next morning the air was limpid and still: a morning on which journeys might very well be started and promises kept. We breakfasted on pancakes and afterwards worked at *Kylie*'s tasks while waiting for wind: Laurence refastening the binocular box more securely to the coaming, Simon re-making joints in the wires to the masthead light, and me renewing the whippings on the tails of the foresail sheets.

Soon after nine the leaves on the ridge began to stir, so Laurence set the mainsail, Simon slipped the buoy, and in half an hour the green spine of Cochino Grande lay behind us. *Kylie* threaded through a dapple of white sand and gingerbread coral, beating towards the palms of Chachahuate.

"Go left a bit."

"Twenty feet . . ."

"Luffing up . . ."

Without an engine it seemed not at all easy to reach Paradise.

"Back the main . . . Hold it . . . Let go . . ."

The anchor dragged, bit, and held. Simon dived overboard and embedded it more firmly. We bagged the foresail, spread the awning and rowed ashore. Again children ran down the hot white beach to prod the dinghy, and above the blue water pelicans faked disasters, crumpling in mid-air like early flying machines, thwacking onto the sea with such violence it seemed impossible that they could survive. Small dark birds, grockles, nodded through the shallows on spindly legs.

"Grockle!" I called to them with gusto. The name had to be spoken to be believed. It sounded centuries older than "arquebus" but did not appear in the *Shorter Oxford*, or *Britannica* or Mencken. Was it in Tolkien? Would Bilbo Baggins have grockled (v.i. Hunted in ankle-deep water with nether garments tucked up)? I couldn't picture him doing it. Aunt Olive might very well grockle in the shallows at Up and Down, but Bilbo wouldn't. Bilbo was into earth, not water.

The palms and *palapas* were exactly as I had remembered them, but youth had moved in; no one in Paradise now was middle-aged. Tomàs Garcia had returned to La Ceiba, along with Michael. Now, a sleek-haired young man named Herbert was in charge at Chachahuate. He danced foxily from foot to foot and talked at high speed. Soon I was the owner of a bag of flour which I had known all along that I'd wanted, as well as a number of coralloid trinkets which I hadn't.

"And that conch over there . . .? The smaller one . . .?"

He put put into my hands a shell which was a subtle blend of colours, from glazed milk-chocolate to sherried cream. I put its bigger end to my lips and blew. It sounded like the bellow of a hungry cow.

"How much?"

"For you, very special price – five dollars."

I gave the conch a second blow and bought it on the spot. If played in concert with another shell already aboard, a shell which gave out a curious noise somewhere between a bleat and a honk, *Kylie*'s entry into Ireland on a foggy morning in July might intrigue walkers on Sheep Head as well as fishermen a mile or two off it, though who would be aboard *Kylie* to blow foghorns apart from myself I didn't yet know; Laurence would be leaving the boat in Florida and Simon was already packing up to go.

145

He lowered his weathered grey backpack into the dinghy and I ferried him to Paradise. Though the island scene was altogether sunny and bright, I felt as if I were transporting him to a very much darker place, for the backpack was the same size as the milestone which used to loom up and burden my spirit whilst cycling homeward from the sanatorium after visiting Pip. "YAR-MTH 25 miles" had said the pocked and mottled legend as I had pedalled bleakly past it against the wind. Now, standing next to Simon's empty black boots on the foreshore, the travel-stained backpack looked like a milestone on the journey to the undiscover'd country from whose bourn no traveller returns.

"Are you quite sure about this?" I said. "Herbert seems a bit shifty."

"M'm? Oh, yeah, I'll give it a try . . .. Beautiful spot!" His eyes were gleaming.

He lugged the backpack up the beach and stood it under a palm tree where the white sand was dirty with wood ash and plastic litter, the edges of which had been bevelled by the sand. Outside a *palapa* a young woman squatted on her haunches, pulled aside a fall of lank hair and smiled at us like Mona Lisa.

"Am going to make myself a rake and tidy things up," Simon said.

"Hey, y'all! Wanna smoke?" said Mona Lisa.

"Wanna smoke?"

23

A Promise in French Harbour

It is well and good if true accounts of voyages under sail mention calm seas and idle canvas, but the picture must not be overdrawn or false expectations may be raised. A calm which takes up more than half a page of print will be read as a coded signal that a leading character is about to suffer violent hurt, or that a serious breach of social order is on the way: at the end of a page-long calm Captain Bligh is obviously going to be deposed by Mr Christian, and the Ancient Mariner's shipmates will drop dead.

For two days *Kylie* drifted among the islands with limp sails. We moored wherever we could to an anchor from bow and stern so as to lie more easily to the awkward swells which sidled round the reefs into the bays. Furtive airs came and went at all hours, like restless creatures in a one-night hotel. We swam and dozed, waiting for a firm wind. The sun blazed down on a glassy sea which heaved and rippled now and then, but the only true waves came from the bows of a motorized dory on its way to Cochino Grande from La Ceiba late on the second afternoon, when Laurence had been sculling for less than half an hour. The dory offered us a tow which, out of pride, we turned down. The sun sank lower and Laurence wiped his forehead. The two sweeps are each ten feet six inches long and Laurence weighs about 160 Imperial pounds. He was putting more beef into the task than I was, but, owing to currents, we were making less than half a knot towards Cochino Grande. I lowered a length of anchor chain over *Kylie*'s bow into the dinghy and rowed it ahead as a tow. After forty minutes of warm labour we had made good another half mile towards the anchorage, but by this time the sun had set.

"Wind," said Laurence tersely from the deck. Above his head a dark shape winged across a darker sky, the last pelican going to its rest.

"Where from?"

"North-west."

"Softly, softly," I felt like saying as the chain clunked back down the navel pipe and Laurence took in the sweeps. We could make out the ridge of Cochino Grande a mile to the north and a glimmer from a house above the bay, but nothing else. The wind was no more than a steady whisper. A stealthy drawing and easing of sheets carried us over the bristly boar into the bay. I steered for the house light, on what I hoped was the bearing of the mooring buoy. The water, twelve feet over the bristly boar, became suddenly deeper. *Kylie* glided though velvet blackness towards the light. Fifty feet of water for a while, then thirty and twenty. When the water had shoaled to twelve feet again we turned away, backed the headsail and shone a flashlight. A pudding-cloth in the water to starboard sprouted wings and took off. A dog barked twice from a verandah. Of the white buoy we saw nothing.

"Please, dog, can we have our ball back?" called out Laurence. The dog barked twice more and the house light went out. We lowered the anchor onto the seabed and hoped it would stay put.

On and off, the calms lasted another five days. Throughout all this time, however, nobody aboard *Kylie* got hurt, and no mutinies of any consequence broke out. I read *Two Gentlemen of Verona* in a single go between porridge and lunch; on the same day Laurence stripped down and re-assembled all three winches.

We digested lobster and drank thin red wine. "According to this," I said, holding up a twenty-year-old *Whitaker's*, "Edinburgh in August witnesses far fewer lunar occultations than Greenwich."

"Eh . . .? What . . .? Are you trying to tell me in a roundabout way that you'll be sailing home via the English Channel?"

"No, I'm still going round the top of Scotland. Fair's fair. Having sailed to New Orleans to give one daughter's hand in marriage, I must do the same in Edinburgh for her sister."

"Lucky she hasn't fallen for an eskimo on the shore of Hudson's Bay."

"That's an interesting thought; most of Hudson's Bay is nearer the Equator than Edinburgh is."

"Thank God for the Gulf Stream, then."

Laurence went below to look for the next bottle. I went back to the almanac. "Gracious! There's only 122 days left till the beginning of August."

"You'll not be in Scotland in time for the wedding at this rate; those oars need to be a foot longer."

He was right. Whether we used the foredeck stanchions or the cockpit winches as crutches, rowlocks, or thole pins, whether we faced forwards and pushed the looms or braced our feet against the coaming and pulled them backwards made no difference to our rate of progress. Whatever we did with the sweeps, *Kylie* went through the water at no more than half a knot.

Like a patient with over-long crutches, *Kylie* tottered across the polished surface of the bay towards the exit. Fortunately for our hands, the calms that day were punctuated by periods of wind. Mostly they were no more than catspaws which crept over the surface and teased the tell-tales before padding off to tickle Bonkes Nose or tease the Lion's Head, but now and then we got something firmer. During half an hour of northerly airs *Kylie* heeled five degrees and glided towards the distant hills of Roatan at four knots; another, stronger breeze from the east carried us five miles on our way. By three in the afternoon we had made good 21 miles and were wallowing stern-on to the reefs at the entrance to the bay in which, weeks before, I had met John Campbell. Laurence lashed the sweeps to the cockpit winches again and tried to turn the bows towards the entrance. As an experiment, I tied a long line to my safety harness, dived in and breast-stoked in the direction in which we wanted to go. Slowly the bows swung round and *Kylie* slid between the reefs. Watched by a pelican, we swam and sculled into Roatan and let fall the anchor.

At the dockside in French Harbour I found out that I was not the only one to lose sleep over the state of his rigging. José Lamas slid a bookmark into *The Road to Oxiana* and put on an ugly grimace. Weeks before on the Rio Dulce, while telling me about the boat he was skippering and the character of its absent owner, he had given a barely perceptible lift of the eyebrow or shoulder to stress a feeling, and slight downbeat of the hand to mark a turn of events. His story had made good listening, even without these helpful signals. Now, having made sure the bookmark was clearly visible, he uplifted both hands and opened them.

"This guy . . .! This owner . . . this *fellow* won't spend any money on his boat! For months I have been telling him that she is falling apart. 'The shrouds are *rotten* . . . You must get me four new shrouds or the mast will come down'." José screwed up his mouth and rattled gravel in his throat. "'Oh, er, are you *sure* . . .? Are you absolutely pozzitiff arbowt that? What will they corst? *Two hunnnerd dollars!* Oh dear, noh, noh, *noh!* You will hev to make do as you are, old chep. Make doo and mend, heh-heh!'"

"The mean devil."

"It's a death trap. You remember that Norther that came through?"

"Yes; we got from Belize to Punta Oeste on it in twenty-three hours. A good wind – twenty-five knots."

"Not stronger?"

"Oh, it blew a gale for two days, but we were in Coxen's Hole by then."

"I am extremely pleased to hear it," said José, "but I was still out in the Bay, coming across from Mario's. A shroud broke . . . and I had some difficulty getting to Utila."

"I can imagine that you did," I said, wondering why stories of other people's misfortunes always lifted my spirits.

I let fall the information that I was sailing to Edinburgh.

"Really?" said José, lifting ever so slightly an eyebrow. "You know, I have a long-standing ambition to attend the Festival . . ."

Before we had quite emptied our beer cans he had asked to sail there in *Kylie*, and I had agreed to it. He would join me in Florida in May, he said, just as soon as he could return the floating coffin to its owner.

That night, I didn't even think about taking tablets. It seemed that things were falling very neatly into place: *Kylie*'s bottom had been painted, her rigging had not been found wanting, and now I had got an agreeable companion to cross the Atlantic with. All that remained to be done before starting on the ocean passage seemed relatively easy: a daysail downwind to Up and Down, then across the wind for a couple of days to the tip of the Yucatàn peninsula, and from there a longer, but none-too-demanding, leg to the east coast of Florida. Sailing eastward against the trade wind across the Gulf of Mexico would be quite bumpy, perhaps, but with the help of the currents Laurence and I could surely do it. The hardest part, I thought, would be finding the currents . . .

For the second time in as few years, I began to compose a wedding speech.

24

Fall of a Swallow

The lobster we devoured in Los Cayos Cochinos was not the largest marine animal ever to grace *Kylie*'s table, but for months afterwards it was the last. Soon after the happy hour at Chachahuate invited us to smoke pot, Laurence and I were eating only meat which, previously, had walked on dry land. It wasn't as though we took a sudden dislike of seafood; it was just that, from the time Simon went off to live in a *palapa*, the hours we spent at sea were given over to catching winds rather than fishes. In the patchy calm which blanketed the Gulf of Honduras, moving a boat which didn't have a motor from one island to the next became a full-time struggle. If, at the end of a stint on the sweeps, *Kylie* ended up alongside a jetty and we trudged ashore in search of some "traditional local seafood", we soon found that the description, like the dishes, had to be taken with a bucketful of salt. As in many other pleasant places where the inhabitants have suddenly found their backyards swarming with lovely tourists, "traditional local seafood" could mean boxed shrimps which had been de-frosted in the next room by an old man in a comical hat.

At the end of an afternoon during which *Kylie* had progressed only yards, I was on the point of asking Laurence if he had ever shot an albatross when a small breeze came in from the east and carried us towards a smoky orange sun, past a sullen reef and into a deep and silent bay. By the time the deck had been tidied we had no desire even to open tins, let alone light the Primus and heat up their often mysterious contents*.

"What I'd *really* like," I remarked wistfully as we plodded through

---

*While stripping labels off canned stores and coding each can with a laundry-marker, a helper back in Southwold had got himself so pleasantly stoned that he had been unable to remember which can was which. Now, years later, I was still opening tins of what was supposedly beef stew and finding they contained rice pudding or, more off-puttingly, mushy peas.

a concourse of mosquitoes, "is a pile of crisp chips straight from the pan, drenched with malt vinegar."

And at the Autostop Pollo, a well-lighted place with shining green plastic tables, this was exactly what I got. In the course of eating a second plateful I could not help thinking back to Saturday nights around the wireless in the thirties, with Mum, Dad and me sitting by the kitchen fire, waiting for the BBC to " . . . stop the mighty . . . (heard by me as 'nightly') . . . roar of London's traffic to bring you . . . (meaning me wiping my plate with a crust, Dad poring over the *Sports Argus*, and Mum lighting a Gold Flake) . . . some of the interesting people who are *In Town Tonight*."

Skewed by longings which get into the thoughts of all travellers far from home, my thoughts expanded into a vision of Aunt Olive, in a centre-parted hairstyle, frying a panful of chips.

Chasing this vision in the only fifteen-knot wind to come our way for a week, we made all of thirty-five miles in eight hours, past Cordelia Reef and Coxen's Hole, towards Up and Down. For me, the visit was also going to be a literary festival. Carried there by *cayucos* or not, the precious English books would have arrived months ago and the classes would surely have prospered. By now, Daphne Howell would be awarding prizes for Reading Aloud, Aunt Olive would be running spelling-bees and Albert would be half-way through *Animal Farm*. To celebrate my visit, they would discharge arquebuses and banquet me on chips.

What happened when I got there was rather different:

SCENE: interior of island shop, midday. Heavy torpor. In shorts, shirt and sun hat, PH appears in up-centre doorway from street and enters.

PH: Hello . . .? *(Louder.)* Mrs Howell . . .?

(He goes to counter, removes hat, cranes into a doorway down left, and coughs.)

PH: Mrs Howell . . .? Shop . . .! MRS HOWELL . . .?

(A Gangly Man, neither old nor young, shuffles in from street. Washed-out cotton trousers, too big for him, are held up by an over-long leather belt. The tail of his shirt is hanging out, his large bony hands hang loosely and his mouth is partly open.)

PH: Is Mrs Howell about?

(Gangly Man gapes wider.)

PH: Mrs Howell . . .? Daphne . . .?

(GM stares intently at PH's hat.)

PH: Ah, yes . . .! *(Takes bottle of cordial from rack, puts coins on counter and makes to leave. G M smiles.)*

(Dissolve to: exterior of island church. Fiddling with its door hasp is Claybourn Howell. Late forties, anxious, flustered, he addresses PH over nearside shoulder.)

Howell: There's only Bibles in there.

PH: When did the classes get started?

Howell: It's a while since I've been over here, so I can't say. To be honest, I don't think they did . . .

PH: I thought the new books would've gingered things up.

Howell: Did you? Did you really . . .?

(We peer over Howell's shoulder into the island's tiny square, eighteen feet by eighteen, bordered by high-backed white benches on which sit four men and two women, each attired in a loose, crinkled garment, off-white or mouse-grey like their skins and hair. To a greater or lesser degree, all their mouths are open. It seems possible that they have been sitting like this for hours.)

(Their faces fade into reflections of sunlight on shallow water, through which plods a grockle.)

Kylie left Up and Down two hours before sunset, beating out between the reefs into a ten-knot breeze from the east. On southerly and westerly courses we cleared the Rocas Salmedina and the Arecife Sur, and soon the small outposts of old England were fading from sight. In spite of the lively chuckles of the waves I felt quite downcast. Rolls-Royces were worth fortunes, but the most valuable vehicle England ever made is its language, and the people of Up and Down were in danger of losing it.

I took hold of the tiller and headed north for Isla Mujeres, off the north-eastern tip of the Yucatán peninsula, three hundred miles away.

By midnight the wind was ENE, twenty-plus knots, and the vane was

Chatting on up.

steering a course of 010° through moderate but irregular seas. From time to time tepid wave-tops dolloped into the cockpit. We reefed the mainsail and put up the working jib. Twelve hours later the wind had veered to east by south and *Kylie* was heading a further twenty degrees to starboard to counteract a strong current setting onto the Banco Chinchorro, the boneyard of ships off the Yucatán coast.

"Ninety-nine miles in twenty hours is five knots, as near as dammit," I remarked at ten past noon, having peeled off a sodden jacket and taken myself below.

"Fair progress," said Laurence from the cockpit.

For me the going was good in other ways too. With Laurence on watch, for the first time in years I could burrow into my sleeping-bag on night passages knowing that *Kylie* was in utterly capable and experienced hands and that, however rumbustious the conditions might be in the cockpit, at the end of my time below I would be woken up with a mugful of tea.

Going back to its earlier form, that afternoon the wind fell light again and backed north-east. That afternoon, too, while writing up the log, I worked out that *Kylie* had covered 25,000 miles since leaving England. In terms of longitude, the figure seemed impossibly high. From the Greenwich meridian to 30°E in the Mediterranean and then westward to the Mississippi delta at 90°W, *Kylie* had sailed only a third of the way round the world, yet, according to my arithmetic, I'd logged more than enough miles to girdle it.

"Your addings-up are probably right," said Laurence. "Think of those hithers and thithers you did in aid of the cruising guide."

"Twenty-five thousand miles seems much too many."

"But you had an engine in those days."

"It would've made no difference to the miles I logged, surely?"

"Perhaps not . . . Anyway, the log could do with a bit of help now – the rotator is hanging vertical."

In spite of the lack of wind and engine we made good 75 miles between one noon and the next, and during the following day, when the wind averaged no more than eight knots, we covered a further 125. Between thirty and forty of these were gained by our being in the North Equatorial Current. Squeezed by Cuba to the north and Mexico to the west, the current was carrying us willy-nilly into the 100-mile-wide Yucatán Channel at nearly two knots.

Before the third sunset of the passage a pair of swallows fluttered about the rigging. Baffled by the motion of the mast and shrouds, after many flustered trials they settled on the guardrail, forward of the mast and as far away from Laurence and me as possible. At sea, flying visitors such as these are not uncommon. Swallows had stayed overnight with Eric and Susan Hiscock aboard *Wanderer IV* during a passage from the Azores to England, when their boat was hove-to, 300 miles from land. Perhaps because North Atlantic weather was colder – or perhaps because they sensed the extraordinary English fondness for wild birds – the Hiscocks' swallows had huddled together in the cockpit so appealingly (" . . . one embracing the other with a protective wing . . .," wrote Eric) that Susan had picked them up in a duster and carried them below to a comfortable bunk. Our visitors had chosen a much warmer evening but we doubted that they could survive, for we had no insects to give them and when daylight came they would still be forty miles from the nearest mosquito.

The coming of a ten-knot breeze shortly before midnight stopped me thinking further about the birds. I set the wind-vane and covered the forehatch, for *Kylie* was now doing five knots and there was a likelihood of spray.

"Steering 005, then," I said when Laurence's eyes had got used to the darkness and my safety harness had been unclipped.

"Be careful where you put yourself," said Laurence; "those birds are down there somewhere – they flew in through the forehatch before you put the lid on it."

In the glow from the chart light I spotted one of our visitors straight away. It had perched on a half-bulkhead, directly above my pillow. I examined the pillowcase and brushed off a small pellet.

"Keep your cards closer to your chest," I told it.

I was woken half an hour earlier than expected by a tickle on my scalp. As a rule, the onset of crawling sensations jerks me bolt upright and sets both hands beating off imagined cockroaches and the like. This time however I kept my body where it was and willed my fingers to investigate. In a very few seconds they were holding the second swallow under the chart light and its eyes were looking up at me. So far as I could see, the little creature was unharmed. Its long pointed wings flexed equally, its eyes were bright and active, and its tiny feet were neatly bunched and tucked. The bird had alighted alongside its mate and had then been tumbled off onto my head by the boat's motion. The bulkhead capping of inch-wide varnished mahogany seemed to be the worst possible resting-place for a bird with such tiny feet, although the slippery surface didn't seem to be troubling its companion.

Sighing, (because it was barely ten minutes till I would be on watch again), I tucked a dry dishcloth into a corner of my sleeping-bag and laid the bird within it.

"Making 5.2 knots close-hauled in a force 2," I wrote at 0400, adding, to Laurence's asperity: "Well done!"

He felt differently, however, during morning twilight. Though since four o'clock I had been off-watch, I had not gone back to my berth, preferring to sit in the cockpit and talk. The dawn was rich with contrasts, the upper air glinting with what looked like slivers of stainless steel, the mainsail glowing like a girl's skin and *Kylie* skimming across a sea of ruffled silk shot with gold. For some minutes we stayed silent, watching the beginning of a new day.

Just before sunrise one of our visitors darted out of the cabin and winged north-westward, making for the invisible land. We craned forward to see it on its way. For a few seconds the wings beat rapidly and the bird sped away truly, at masthead height above the sea; but after only a hundred yards the beats faltered and the little body spiralled downwards like a scrap of charred paper to disappear among the waves. Though its death had been expected much earlier, (such visitors live only about four hours, we had agreed), the manner of it came as a shock. Repeating incompletely the words of Dylan Thomas, I had said that fatigue and hunger would ensure that the birds wuld go gentle into that good night, but it seemed that this little creature was not giving up without a fight. Starving, weak, feathers clogged with water, the swallow struggled out of the sea, into the air and the first rays of the sun. It fluttered between sky and sea, bathed in light, fighting on against the odds. The contest brought Laurence to his feet, one hand gripping the sprayhood and the other pointing. I felt like cheering. And then suddenly, just when the swallow seemed to be gaining height, it fell a second time, dropping like a shuttlecock onto the shining floor. The little drama was ended: this time the swallow was gone for good.

Laurence sat down and turned his face to the sun. I unzipped my jacket and went below. The other bird was lying stiff-legged in the dishcloth where I had put it. I palmed the body, slipped it overboard and closed my eyes, thinking that when all was said and done, if there was indeed a special providence in the fall of a sparrow, it was likely that the same thing went for a swallow.

Having noted down these happenings, I got out a knife and asked Laurence if he would like a grapefruit for his breakfast.

25

To Florida

Making six knots over the seabed to a fifteen-knot north-easterly wind, *Kylie* came up to Isla Mujeres and anchored in one-and-a-half fathoms off the south beach. We thought to lie there for a day or so in hope of catching a better slant for the Florida Strait. I hung up the oil lamp on the forestay and Laurence made tea. Having drunk it, we got our heads down; and were woken too soon after daybreak by the thunderous noise of the island garrison setting off on its daily jog, bellowing patriotic slogans as it went. The idea of puttting up with another dawn chorus of this nature did not appeal to us, so in fierce sunshine and hampered yet again by a calm, we towed *Kylie* half a mile southwards to the Marina Paraiso. It was lucky that we moved from the anchorage when we did, and even luckier that we berthed *Kylie* close astern of a bulky coaster, for in the early hours of the next morning Isla Mujeres was struck by the fiercest north-westerly gale in sixty years. It quickly transformed the trade-wind anchorage into a lee shore. Several yachts dragged anchor and collided, and in the marina four others were heavily battered against the jetty by steep waves. Though the wind was too violent for *Kylie* to be setting out offshore, nevertheless it was blowing from the right direction. Sheltered from the worst of the wind and waves by the coaster, we renewed the frapping on the docklines and waited. By eleven o'clock the wind had eased, and someone had picked his way through the dockside debris to bring us the latest weatherfax. It said that the vigorous cold front presently south of the island would be followed by another from the north-west during the following day. However, this next front would be weaker, its isobars spaced at wider intervals, and no further strong winds were expected during the next forty-eight hours. We might see no better forecast than this for weeks. I decided to leave at once.

The unyielding trio of Port Captain, Customs and Immigration saw to it that we did not get away so very quickly. Not till half-past twelve was the last document signed and delivered. An hour later *Kylie* hurried past the island's candy-striped lighthouse into the Yucatán Channel and shaped a course for the first of the Florida Keys, 350 miles away.

To make this passage at a decent speed and in not too much discomfort we needed moderate winds from any point more than fifty degrees away from north-east. We also needed to find an east-going branch of the Gulf Stream current and stay in it – a task which is not as easy as it looks from the chart. After passing through the Yucatán Channel, the warm equatorial current fans out across the Gulf in a number of streams, one of which flows towards Florida. However, from time to time masses of water detach themselves from the mainstream to eddy aimlessly among the cooler waters, and so, although the general flow of this stream is easterly, it is quite possible for a boat to be carried off in a contrary direction by an eddy.

The wind stayed west of north for only eight hours. From time to time we threw a bucket over the side and sampled the sea. If its temperature were to fall below 27°C we would know we had strayed out of the current. Although for hour after hour the thermometer showed that the sea was 27.5°C, and although, too, we were sailing well free of close-hauled, the satnav recorded that *Kylie* was making good no more than five knots over the ground.

We covered eighty miles in this unspeedy but comfortable manner. The wind then veered again and headed us, blowing strongly enough for two reefs, allowing *Kylie* to point no closer than forty-five degrees to the course. For four days she plunged through waves which got a little larger by the hour, close-hauled on the starboard tack when the wind veered east, and on port tack when it swung back to NE, under the genoa or the working jib when it was blowing force five or six but latterly under only the small storm jib and deep-reefed main when it rose to force seven.

Finding, on the fourth day, that we had made good only fifty-five miles in twenty-four hours, we eased sheets, wrung out our neck towels and went below for a mugful of tea. The ocean was grey and gloomy, and the cabin not much better. While waiting for the kettle to come to the boil, Laurence remarked that the wind was now all of twenty-five knots and rising. I pulled on my last dry jersey and bent over the chart. We had been pushed fifty miles north of our intended track by adverse winds and eddies. To get back into the east-going mainstream we would sail south, I said stoutly, encouraged perhaps by the strength of the tea and the warmth of the jersey to gloss over the fact that if we found the current, the strong wind blowing against it would certainly make the already steep waves much steeper. Laurence blew onto his tea and sipped it. Then he took up a pencil and drew a weather-map based on a radio forecast which to me had been inaudible and declared that the only way to get into a better slant of wind was to stay on the starboard tack, heading NNE. Also, he went on with growing ardour, this heading would take us into the lee of the western coast of Florida, where the waves would be smaller . . .

" . . . and where our present discomfort would end," was a thought he left unsaid, but one with which I would have agreed. It was impossible to know which of these courses of action was right, so in the end we left the deciding vote to the wind; if it blew from the NE we would head towards Cuba; if it veered south of east we would head for Key West.

Throughout the night and the following morning we struggled to match deeds to words, tacking straight away when the wind shifted, and changing headsails according to its strength, setting the number two genoa during the occasional patches of moderate wind, clawing it down and lashing it to the guardrail before setting the working jib when the seas became steeper and larger, and then, sometimes less than an hour later, when *Kylie* was plunging into a force seven and the seas were larger still, clambering forward to set up the storm jib and bundle the other sail into its bag. In between these activities we would cast a bucket over the side and take the sea temperature, a more delicate business, but one which by then had become a necessary ritual to ensure we got to the happier world which lay – according to testimonies of mariners gone before but not forgotten – somewhere on the far side of Key West. Soon the bucket had become a chalice and the thermometer an icon, hidden away when not in use, safe from the eyes of the common herd. Now, held gingerly in the liquid sloshing around in the bucket, then held aloft in the bright moonlight or – more often – torchlight to display the coloured thread in the narrow tube, the figure 27 became an obsession, rather like the pass mark in an exam.

These doings did not get us very far. Only twenty miles had been made good, said the satnav, in sixteen hours. At which rate, remarked Laurence, it was going to take us another five days to get to Key West.

"Very well," I said when my last remaining jersey was soaked through, "let's head for Tampa instead."

So we eased the sheets a little, and thirty-six hours later were flying the green-and-red spinnaker in Tampa Bay.

26

José

Thirty miles from the open sea and tucked neatly into the north-east corner of Tampa Bay, the Davis Island Yacht Club offers the tired sailor a sheltered berth and first-rate hospitality. Indeed, so far as the visitor who wants to sail to the United Kingdom as soon as possible can make out, the Club's only fault is that it lies on the wrong coast. To get his boat to a better place from which to begin a transatlantic passage, he will have to go round or across hundreds of miles of peninsular Florida. Even if he makes the roundabout journey non-stop and is carried ninety miles on his way by currents, it looked to Laurence and me like being a three-day job at the least.

The other route, economical in miles but probably less so in hours and certainly not so in dollars, required the hire of an outboard engine and motor-sailing across the state to the Atlantic Ocean via Lake Okeechobee and the Intracostal Waterway. A third way, *infra dig* but the one which I chose, was to have *Kylie* hauled across Florida by road. This turned out to be less costly than expected and was done in under a day; the boat was trucked away from Tampa after breakfast, and by teatime I was pumping-up the Primus in a boatyard at Fort Pierce, a harbour on almost the same parallel of latitude but 130 miles nearer Ireland.

By 1st May the jobs list had been whittled down from the middle teens to six. Laurence was determined to get the figure down to nil. Sweating a little, he put to rights the masthead lantern, which had been knocked askew by the overhead cable in Roatan like the extortionist in the flowery shirt had said it would be, and as good as rewired the mast in the course of a single afternoon. As defence against a wave of the size which John Campbell had met with, I re-bolted the plywood deadlights over the cabin windows. In theory the deadlights cut down by 70% the amount of light which came in but, because the curtains were usually kept drawn, in practice they made no difference to what I could see in the cabin twilight. The act of re-fixing the deadlights st have benefited my subconscious, for after doing it I went to sleep without tablets for three nights in a row.

At lighting-up time on the fourth day the russet sky suddenly vanished, as usual, and the boatyard became a maritime tableau, with *Kylie* the floodlit centrepiece. We put our tools away and tramped into town to eat pizzas in a place which, apart from its air-conditioning and bustle, was not unlike an eating-house I knew in County Cork. I said

". . . don't start out from here."

as much to Laurence as we looked for a table, adding that when I reached Ireland I intended to eat there once again.

"If you're sailing to Ireland by way of Bermuda," said a long-nosed man with salt-and-pepper hair who was preparing to fork into a fifteen-inch pizza on the other side of the table at which eventually we sat, "then you don't start out from here."

"No?"

"You need to get yourself five hundred miles north before heading east. No-one ever makes it to Bermuda by tryin' to sail straight there from Fort Pierce."

Laurence lifted a polystyrene cup and drank. The fork circum-navigated the plate opposite and prodded an anchovy lying at seven o'clock.

"There's Fort Pierce, right?"

I nodded, and the fork dinted straight across sliced green pepper and mushroom until it was targeting a central tomato.

"That's Bermuda."

"Yes," I said, inspecting a medium-sized Margharita which had been set down in front of me.

"You won't ever get there by goin' straight for it, because on that route there's no wind to speak of."

"None?"

"Not a breath."

At this point in our exchanges I understood why the Greeks had made a habit of shooting messengers.

"All right, then; so what about going with the Gulf Stream as far as Savannah . . .?"

"No, you got to go further."

"Charleston?"

"*Furrther!*" The fork jabbed at a peripheral red pepper at ten o'clock. "You need to be as far north as Morehead City. Don't even *think* about making a right till you're sideways to Cape Hatteras."

I contemplated my pizza, which by then was looking rather more than I could manage. The man was remorseless. As well as the dreadful shortage of wind, he went on, the direct course from Fort Pierce to Bermuda would plunge me into bigger problems.

"Such as weed . . .?" I said, squeezing my cup and cracking a thin smile.

"Weed will be the least of them." He put down his fork and bent towards me till the tip of his nose was above the edge of my

Margharita. "You'll run into *electrical* problems – radio blackouts – *an' your compass will go crazy.*"

"M'm, yes," said Laurence, who till that moment had seemed to be taking in only what he was eating. "Some aeroplanes – Grummann Martlets, I think – were lost near Bermuda during the War."

"That's right – whole flight of them vanished."

"What an elevating chat," said Laurence when we had walked back to the boatyard and were about to climb *Kylie*'s ladder, "but you would need to have a bit of a think before asking him to share your cockpit."

Seconds after saying this he called down that the vacancy had been filled already. I clattered up the ladder. A backpack and a sleeping-bag were in the cockpit. On top of the backpack lay an open book.

"As I was saying . . .," said Laurence.

"He's here," I said, with a smile which this time was unforced, looking at *The Road to Oxiana.*

José came up the ladder soon afterwards, and by noon on 8th May I had crossed off the last item on the jobs list. *Kylie*, it seemed, was ready for sea. The dinghy had been lashed down, the water cans topped up and the kettle filled. The chart had been opened and the barometer fiddled with until its hand was in line with the coastguard's reading of 1017 mbs. José stowed *Oxiana* above his berth and wedged it in with a cushion.

It was a fine, clear day, cloudless over the land but with a grey fleece far out to the east above the Gulf Stream, and a light westerly wind. Boats glided past the dockside, heading out with the wind and tide. José sat on the coachroof under the awning, watching them. Laurence loaded his bags into a hired car and studied a road map. In spite of these signals of early departure I felt no strong urge to cast off, for the day was a Friday. Once before I had set out on a long passage on a Friday and soon afterwards had run into atrocious weather.

Laurence parked the car in the shade of a tree. After a minute or two of fiddling with its switches, he locked the car and came back to the dockside, beaming.

"'Wind ten to fifteen knots, falling to ten knots overnight', it says."

"Oh, yes?"

"'Seas two feet'."

I knocked ash from my pipe.

"Couldn't be better," said Laurence.

"That's what you said when we left Isla Mujeres."

"Ha-ha."

"Won't be a lot different tomorrow or the day after, though, will it?"

"Hardly likely."

A Sparkman and Stephens sloop went past with its spinnaker drawing nicely. José hummed a stirring tune. I put away my pipe.

"Let's get the awning off, then," I said.

José got to his feet, Laurence had cast off the shorelines and I was thinking again about the course to take.

According to the Pilot Chart of the North Atlantic for May 1988, the man with pepper-and-salt hair had been largely right. Though riding the Gulf Stream only as far north as Savannah would bring me into an area of ocean in which 56% of winds came from the western half of the compass, by going with the Stream a further 300 miles to the latitude of Morehead City the interloper would advance two hundred miles nearer Bermuda. Assisted by a two-knot current, his much longer route would be faster than mine by one-and-a-half days. He seemed to have been wrong, though, about the likelihood of calms. According to the chart, the chances of running into a calm on either route were 3%, which struck me as being comparatively low*. And even if I angled out of the Gulf Stream and tried to sail a straight-line course to Bermuda, the chances of a calm became no higher than 4%.

But the figures were " . . . averages obtained from data gathered over many years . . .," said the chart, " . . . not intended to be used alone but in conjunction with other navigational aids". A sextant and a thermometer, for example. Thinking this, I crabbed into the axis of the Gulf Stream in the late afternoon with the idea of going with it at least as far as Savannah; and José cooked an early dinner. Before we could eat it the sun had disappeared behind a tall bulbous cloud which had loomed up from behind low grey battlements. I noted down the barometer reading and beside it wrote an exclamation mark in closed brackets. Either something had gone wrong somewhere or it was about to. Set at 1017 mbs at seven that morning, the barometer had plummetted to 982.

"The seven o'clock reading must be wrong," I said to José; "I must have mis-heard the coastguard." This was a lie. How was it possible for even me to mistake hearing "Nine hundred . . ." as "One thousand . . ." when their vowel sounds were so different?

---

* And still does. The chart records the same 3% of calm in the Western Approaches to the English Channel, as against 6% calm in the North Sea off Lowestoft, 8% in the Mediterranean off Turkey and a truly dispiriting 12% between Corsica and France.

The wind had fallen lighter but was still westerly. José brought the pocket radio into the cockpit and tried for a weather forecast, but all he could hear were fervent prayers from a station in Georgia and a series of ethereal clucks. The weather channel on the walkie-talkie gave out similar clucks, accompanying them with loud belches.

Sunset was always a very awkward time of day for radios, we said.

So far, the satnav did not seem to be affected. According to its figures, *Kylie* was making five-and-a-half knots in spite of the smallness of the wind, and was tracking 005°.

I squeezed detergent into a half-bucketful of seawater, washed two spoons and two dishes and regarded the sky. Below a narrow streak of white the clouds were drooping like sodden jerseys. Suddenly, lightning pulsed within them, and the wind strengthened and veered ten degrees north. *Kylie* heeled slightly to starboard. Though no stronger than twelve knots, already the northing in the wind was steepening the waves.

I uncleated the tiller lines, eased the sheets and turned forty degrees eastward. Soon after I had done this, the wind shifted to WNW and the seas became fidgety. José tried for a weather forecast, again without success. The satnav stated that Bermuda bore 075°, 820 miles distant. I dipped the saucepan into the bucket and, while scouring it, noticed that its handle was loose. I dried my hands, wrote "Saucepan" in a corner of the log sheet and looked at the chart. Riding a two-knot Gulf Stream would be all very well in southerly or westerly winds and settled weather, but if the wind were to blow strongly against the current we should be in danger. There came another flash of lightning and the wind veered NNW. The wavetops fluttered testily, like starlings fighting over crumbs. I emptied the bucket among them and steered 075°, out of the axis of the Stream, on a straight line for Bermuda.

In spite of the day being a Friday and the none-too-helpful omens from the sky and sea, I was happy. Whether the auguries are good or bad, there is always a special excitement about leaving the land, and I was feeling it strongly now. *Kylie* had sailed hundreds of miles of the New World's shoreline, much of which had been interesting and some of which had been beautiful; but now, making out into the ocean at right angles to the shore, I was glad to turn my back on it. As a boy, it had been the difference in feeling between the long-drawn-out pleasure of walking up the side of the old Bull Ring in Birmingham, where shops with galoshes or pigs' heads or tubes of sweet sherbet held your eyes, and the acidulous delight of darting away from the gas lamps, across the cobblestones into the dark.

At six next morning a hard-eged line of black cloud bore down on us from the north. We reefed the mainsail, made a flask of soup and recorded that the barometer had risen to 1002 mb. As the front passed over and swept southwards, the wind rose to twenty knots and veered north for a while before swinging back north-west. By noon we were out of the Gulf Stream, having made good 90 miles in 19 hours from Fort Pierce, but the barometer was falling again. I noted the fall without comment, for if a strong northerly were to come upon us now the seas would be much less dangerous.

At four in the afternoon we handed the mainsail and winged-out the genoas to light westerly airs. A small bird with red stripes in its wings flew out of the setting sun to gorge on insects lodged in the creases of the mainsail and the crannies of the rigging. I drilled-out the remains of a corroded rivet from the saucepan handle, replaced it with a nut and bolt and set down the pan on the stove with a small flourish.

"That looks promising," said José from the cockpit. Above the berths, the netting bags swung gently, bulging with fruit and vegetables.

I lifted out a green one and said "Zucchini?"

"Right first time! Give yourself a merit mark."

I sharpened the galley knives and prepared a more elaborate meal than I would have done if had been cooking only for myself. The presence of someone else is always a spur to do things extra well, and with José aboard it seemed even more necessary, what with English cookery being a standing joke on mainland Europe. There was also the fact that this, the first meal of the transatlantic passage, had to set a standard for future reference. "How about . . .," I saw myself saying from my sleeping-bag in light-to-moderate seas on the way to the Azores, " . . . another Chicken Kiev . . .?"

For an hour I chopped vegetables, sifted flour, beat eggs, fried chicken and stirred saucepans. We ate the result in the cockpit, the evening fine and clear, a quarter moon gleaming, its image scattered by a ruffled sea.

"Very good," said José, laying down his plate.

"Really?" I was not putting it on. José had travelled three continents and his father was a member of the Diplomatic Corps. I pictured them ordering quails' eggs from Fortnum's and spooning caviare with the Papal nuncio.

"Yes, it was excellent."

"Thanks very much," I said, stepping over two dirty saucepans, a frying pan and a greasy bucketful of galley implements on the way to my berth. "Barometer's settled down, it seems. See you at a quarter-to-midnight. Tea with one sugar, please."

By then the wind had swung into the east and fallen light, and José had re-set the mainsail. Though logging 80 miles in the previous 24 hours, on that day we made good only 52. It was followed by days of 67, 104, 88 and 57 miles. The "Remarks" column in the logbook, which usually contained only details of the changes in weather, sea-state and sails, was invaded by tidings of death and disaster: the finding of the shrivelled corpse of a finch under a sailbag in the forepeak, and the sighting of a capsized speedboat. The speedboat wallowed in the swell like a slaughtered whale, its lacerated white belly upturned and awash. Hovering near it were two sharks. We eased the sheets and pondered. Should we thump on the hull and put an ear to it in case a hand within tapped "S.O.S.", or hammer holes in it till it sank?

The sharks idled towards *Kylie*, attended by wriggling scavengers.

"Three metres," said José, eyeing the sharks.

"Longer: fifteen feet, I'd say."

The sharks hung twenty yards astern, fins barely moving. We looked at the wreck more closely.

"Look, it's got barnacles growing on its topsides; it must have capsized months ago."

I hardened the sheets and *Kylie* gathered way.

"We should report it," said José. But how, and to whom? We were more than a hundred miles from land and no other ships were in sight; the walkie-talkie would be useless.

We went back on course for Bermuda. The sharks took up station astern and followed.

I cooked more dinners, some as ambitious as the first, and each trailing its washing-up. José went on paying compliments about my cooking and staying politely silent about the clutter of dirty pans and dishes that came with it. However, the intervals between the finish of a meal and the start of the dish-washing grew longer. At eleven o'clock on the ninth night at sea I came into the cockpit to find the pans still in the bucket.

I delivered a brisk homily.

"H'm. I'm afraid there's been a slight accident."

"Oh?"

"The sponge has gone over the side."

"No!"

"I'm sorry."

"But . . . but . . . but I'd had that sponge *five years*."

"Really? I do apologise."

"I got it in the Greek islands, at Kalymnos."

"I feel really terrible about it."

"Twenty drachmae, it was."

"Oh, dear! I'm just a butterfingers."

"Yes. All right." I groped in the back of a locker and pulled out a plastic foam creation the size of a housebrick. "You'd better use this. It's far too big to wash up with, so I'll cut it in half. It won't be as good as the one you have lost, mind, but it'll have to do."

Next morning the wind was mainly north-east, ten knots or less. By noon we had sailed 700 miles. With 250 still to go and the wind light and adverse, the passage could take another week. During the afternoon the satnav let on that it was unable to fix our position, and so, while José oiled the Walker's log and streamed it, I prepared another dinner.

"We need to get this lot inside us before twilight," I remarked, stirring a panful of curried beef.

"Yes."

"Can't have the cockpit cluttered while taking a star sight, can we?"

"Of course not!"

Minutes after sunset we laid aside our dishes. I gazed aloft, looking for the first star.

"That was delicious," said José, leaning back against the coaming and putting his feet up.

"Why are you putting your feet up?"

"I want to think about Nargiz."

"Who's she?"

"It's the Persian for 'narcissus' and, according to Byron*, the same name is used in Aramaic and Armenian. Isn't that remarkable . . .?"

"Yes . . . but what about the washing-up?"

"And – listen! – wait a minute! – what is even more astonishing is that the Chinese word for narcissus, *nargiz*, is *nai-ki* . . ."

"Really? And what's the Spanish for 'dishes'?"

José lowered his feet onto the duckboard and peered into the cabin.

---

*Robert Byron, author of *The Road to Oxiana* (1937).

"They can stay in soak a little longer, I think; the satnav has come back to life again."

I went to my berth, lit the cabin lamp and left him to it. *Kylie* heeled to port a few degrees and stayed there, and for the first time in days I heard the swish of water against the hull and the click of the winch pawls as the sheet was firmed. The wind held. *Kylie* kept going at a small but steady pace, nodding now and then to a wave. I settled my shoulders and began to read a short history of Bermuda. Before long, I heard the clatter of dishes being washed. I plumped up a cushion and turned a page.

"Oh, dear!"

My head was out of the companionway in an instant. "What? Not again?"

He was leaning over the guardrail, the upturned bucket in his hand. "You *haven't . . .*?"

"Yes, I have."

"Bloody hell!"

"I'm most terribly sorry."

"Stop it! Just stop it!"

"I'll buy another one in Bermuda."

"Go to the devil."

Morning came, and the wind lighter. Tea was made dutifully but drunk in silence. I came out to find him handing the Walker log.

"Weed," he said. "Sargassum."

"Yes."

"Making no better than 080 in the past hour."

"No."

He went below and turned in. One-hundred-and-seventy-six to go. The wind backed NNE. I handed the genoa and put up the ghoster. By eleven o'clock we were logging 3.5 knots and there was a small tumble of foam under the bows. I sat on the pulpit with my back to the wind and looked upward. The ghoster was a shimmering triangle, gossamer-light, soft to the fingers but stronger than they were, bowing at its edges to the wind and puckering at its corners with the strain. More than ever that morning, I marvelled at the way the sail was yielding to the wind and yet was gaining from it too.

I latched-in the steering vane at the sixth notch and crept down to the galley. José pulled his sheet over his face and turned to the wall. I broke four eggs into a basin and beat them.

Half an hour later he spooned the last morsels of scrambled egg into his mouth and slid his plate into the bucket. Now I was in a quandary. If I went below without mentioning them, the dishes might very well stay in the bucket until teatime, in which case I would have a fit. On the other hand, to point out yet again that we were down to our last, albeit inferior, synthetic sponge might plunge us back into the terrible cataleptic silence out of which, over grapefuit, tomatoes and scrambled eggs, we had only just begun to emerge.

"Going to get my head down for a while." I stepped over the washing-up and sat in my berth. "This Byron book, what's it like?"

"Quite good."

"Have you finished it?"

"No, but it doesn't matter. Make a start if you like."

"*Venice, August 20th, 1933 [I read] . . .. The bathing, on a calm day, must be the worst in Europe: water like hot saliva, cigarette-ends floating into one's mouth, and shoals of jelly-fish.*"

Ten pages on, I put my head out of the cabin with the intention of telling him how good it was and slipping in an enquiry about the dishes. What I saw defeated me.

"You . . .! You've . . .! It's . . . ho-ho!"

José stopped what he was doing and regarded me severely. "Why are you holding your sides? Something wrong?"

"And . . . and . . . it's . . . ho-ho!" I got out, pummelling a cushion; " . . . it's not just twine . . . ha-ha! . . . b-b-bbut ro-!"

"I really do think you ought to go back to taking those tablets."

Byron fell to the cabin sole. I collapsed into my berth. José had attached the sponge to his wrist. The rope was half an inch thick.

27

Strong Wind off Bermuda

A narrow white triangle showed up on the horizon astern. The binoculars were passed back and forth between us. Was she a sloop, a ketch or a cutter? Though pointing closer to the light airs than we were, the oncoming boat could only be heading for Bermuda, a hundred and ten miles away at the last reckoning; but where had she come from? Larger than *Kylie* by far, in an hour she overtook us a quarter of a mile abeam. Nobody was visible on deck. Unlike *Kylie*, she carried weathercloths in way of the cockpit. Perhaps the watchkeeper was peering at us through a slit. Why on earth didn't he put up a hand and wave?

"Surely he can't be below deck all this time!"

"Why not? Somebody might have bid Three No Trumps with only twelve points in his hand."

"She must be making all of five knots."

"It's a very quiet engine," said José. "Do you hear it?"

"No."

"She'll be *there* tomorrow."

"But think of the noise below deck," I said happily; "I bet they haven't slept a wink."

"M'm."

"Look. Isn't that a head sticking up?"

"No, it's a dan buoy."

Not until the other boat had drawn ahead and was forty degrees past our beam did I pick up the walkie-talkie.

"*Magic Carpet*. Left Saint Augustine nine days back," we heard faintly through the crackle.

"Switch over to High Power and report the wrecked speedboat," José said.

I did as he suggested but, though *Magic Carpet* was no more than a mile away by then, we heard no reply.

That night, rain filled the water cans to overflowing, and at four in

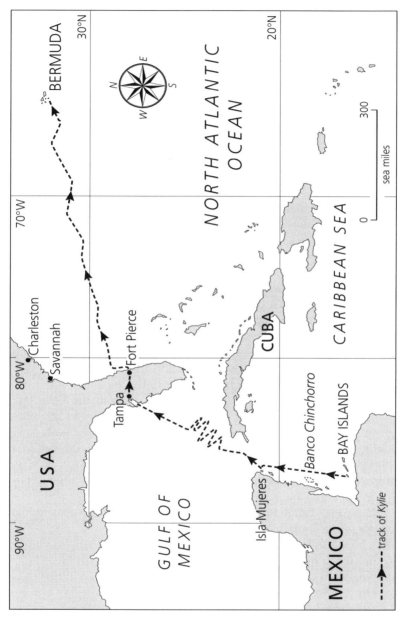

Chart 7: Caribbean Sea and North Atlantic Ocean:
Bay Islands to Bermuda.

Sailing Home

the morning the wind started to blow with authority. It was dead against us, but we loved it.

"Six miles in the hour," I said as we took in the first reef at the change of watch. "At this rate we could be . . ."

"Don't *say* it . . .," cut in José; "you mustn't say it!"

"Waypoint 1: 073° x 67.6'," I wrote in the log. The waypoint was 10 miles south of the western end of the Bermudas, and Waypoint 2, off the port of St George's, was 20 miles farther.

By eight the wind was twenty-five knots and the lee sidebench was streaming water for minutes together; by ten the wind was gusting thirty knots. There was no question of separate watches now; the boat needed us both. We backed the jib and deep-reefed the main.

"Reef the jib too," I said when the mainsheet had been hardened a little and the points tied. The jib had been bought new in Florida. In the sail loft its whiteness had not looked especially brilliant. Now, against the murk of the storm clouds, it looked like an advert for Procter & Gamble.

Splayed on the foredeck, we beat it into a stiff roll and shackled the luff cringle to the deck strop.

"You, halyard; me, cockpit."

The luff ran up the forestay as quick as a ferret. I sheeted in till the leech stopped snapping, then waited till José had made up the halyard before taking in more sheet on the winch.

"Good wind," he said, clambering back to the cockpit.

Storm boards in place, spray-dodger tied back to the horse, we plunged forward again, with Bermuda somewhere beyond the blue-green hills which rose and broke one after the other on the bow.

Hunched under the sprayhood we ate chocolate and drank coffee. I emptied a puddle from my pocket and struggled to light a pipe. Apropos of nothing that had gone before, José broached the subject of his friend Phil, who, he said, had been caught growing cannabis.

"Carry on," I said, folding down the top leaf of the washboards and groping for a dry lighter; "I'm still listening . . ."

" . . . and so he's had to get out . . ."

"What, out of town?"

"No, out of the country."

"Oh . . .! So where's he gone to?"

"Bermuda."

The wind eased a little but *Kylie* still laboured, the foresail rattling and snatching as she reared and plunged.

174

I latched-in the steering vane and José went below. Suddenly the morning was filled with Radio Bermuda. I closed the storm boards and pumped dry the bilge.

José's hand came out, holding a mug of tea. "It's blowing like this for miles. A cruise liner has been lying-to off St George's all morning, waiting a chance to get in."

The liner was still lying-to at sunset. We glimpsed it through gouts of spray. Bermuda was a dribble of green stew on a crumpled napkin and the liner a black beetle sucking at it. The scene was lit from below by a ghastly light which seeped through the clouds and oozed over the horizon, tingeing everything a bilious yellow.

"I just can't manage a Chicken Kiev, I'm afraid . . ."

By midnight the wind was down to fifteen knots. At one-thirty we hove-to in the green sector of St David's Head light. The walkie-talkie was dead and the dishes had not been washed up, but between the narrow cliffs at the entrance shone the lights of the harbour.

Having taken 13 days 6 hours to sail 1072 miles, we unlashed the anchor and went in.

28

Coldfinger

ice . . . *a crystalline form of the drug methylamphetamine
or "speed", smoked . . . for its stimulant effects.*

Oxford Dictionary of New Words (1991)

Hotel marmalade dribbled from underdone toast and blotted out
Featherbed Alley. I wiped clean the tourist brochure and went on
eating.

"A week out from Fort Pierce it came on worse than ever and lasted
longer," said José.

I pushed a cream jug across the table towards his coffee cup. "I think
it could've been that very first Chicken Kiev," I said; "the peas were
six years old."

We were eating a late breakfast under a green-and-white striped
awning on the south-western side of King's Square at St George's, a
part of the town with many reminders of its colonial past, including a
well-varnished replica of a seventeenth-century pillory into which a
cruise-line passenger was putting his head. A camera flashed.

"I feel that I'm letting you down," said José in a level tone. *He's
letting his coffee go cold, too . . .*, muttered my father from the depths
of Featherbed Alley; " . . . *and* him a *Spaniard . . .*"

"Don't talk barmy," I said. "The thing is, what'll *you* do?" Crew
were not allowed to sign-off ships in Bermuda unless they had another
berth to go to, or airline tickets home.

"I'll ask around," said José, still not picking up the cream jug.

Two women in cinnamon-and-tangerine tee-shirts pulled the tourist
out of the pillory and bundled him towards the stocks. " . . . contrivances
designed for the humiliation of erring citizens," added the brochure.

Knees bent and back cricked, I wiped kerosene soot from *Kylie's*
deckhead, working the cleaning-rag into the crannies. After half an
hour of it I went to the cockpit to straighten my back, thinking with

176

dismay that claustrophobia must be awful. To me the cabin was a snug workplace, with a rack for the pencil and dividers above the chart table on the one hand, and the Primus stove with its dented aluminium kettle coming to the boil only two feet away on the other. The compactness of the cabin meant that *Kylie* was a less damaging container for a person to be in when tossed around by heavy seas; larger cabins meant bigger bruises. Above all, to me *Kylie*'s cabin was a haven; to José, however, it had seemed like a tomb.

"Oyez!" cried a man with a spade ginger beard, scarlet coat, three-cornered hat and large handbell. "Be it known . . . at the pleasure of His Excellency . . . a symphonic concert!"

The Bermuda Philharmonic Orchestra filtered into the square, their sombre jackets and formal dresses at odds with the tangerine tee-shirts in the crowd; hair pulled back, smiling quite tightly but eager to give a lot. An oboe called twice and then the orchestra launched into *Pomp and Circumstance*, carrying my thoughts with it, up over the signal station into a damson sky, my ears straining all the while to hear the high notes. Pip was in the square too, only inches away from me but beyond reach. She was nodding in time with the music. Her lips were parted but nothing came from them.

Upstairs in O'Malley's pub José told me that he had found a berth in another boat, along with Phil. The boat was seventy feet in length, its cabin fourteen feet wide, and was sailing to Barcelona via the Azores.

"Good for *you*," I said, really meaning it in spite of the perilous amplitude of his new accommodation. "Good for you *both*."

A beaming shopkeeper with waxed points to his moustache sold me a pound of St Bruno Flake tobacco and three jars of extra-thick marmalade in which my knife might easily stand upright, he said, till the Last Trump; and the harbourmaster gave me, without charge, a sheaf of weather maps. They showed a vast area of high pressure stretching north-eastward from the Azores to the English Channel and south-westward to Florida. *Kylie*'s passage to Bermuda had been slow, but, according to the harbourmaster, other boats had been slow too, hampered by the same mixture of light winds and adverse gales whether they had come to Bermuda from Morehead City or from Florida.

I rolled up the canvas cover of the book rack in the forepeak and looked into the past. Printed in 1963, Hiscock's *Voyaging Under Sail* recorded that *Moonraker* had got from Bermuda to the Azores in 20 days on her 29-ft waterline, and that *Wanderer III* had taken 14 days to sail from the Azores to Falmouth. Both boats were bigger than *Kylie*, so it seemed likely that getting to Ireland via the Azores might take me forty days at least – rather too long a time for somebody wanting to drink Guinness in County Cork early in July. Seeing these passage-times, I decided to give the Azores a miss.

The pilot books were in two minds about the best eastbound sailing route from Florida to Britain. Findlay in 1848 had advocated the Azores route as being much safer and sometimes faster, whereas the route prescribed in the 1973 edition of the Admiralty's *Ocean Passages for the World* lay far to the north of the islands. However, the Admiralty's route was meant for " . . . large sailing vessels, able to stand up to, and take advantage of, the heavy weather to be expected . . .," and was preceded by a caution about ice.

I put away wonderful Hiscock and the extra-thick marmalade and got out the *Pilot Chart for the North Atlantic* for June 1988. From Newfoundland and Nova Scotia a broken red line marking the mean maximum iceberg limit stretched far south-eastwards into the Atlantic. It looked like the outline of a hand which had had its middle fingers cut off at their bottom joints.

The Admiralty route lay across the knuckles, far inside the iceberg limit. But, for all its appearance of very modern menace, the charted iceberg limit was an historical abstraction based on centuries of statistics. What with the effects of global warming and the abnormal behaviour of El Niño, the Holy Child current in the Pacific, an outline of the ice in the North Atlantic in June 1992 might look very different from the red hand of 1988.

José came out of the forehatch of the seventy-footer, clutching a pair of wire-cutters and a diagram which looked like a map of the London Underground.

"We're installing two k's worth of electronics," he said, snipping busily. "What're you up to?"

"Shopping for a 4B chart pencil and a set of batteries for the walkie-talkie."

On the way back I called in at the Harbour Office on Ordnance Island for a weather forecast. The lobby was filled with earnest giants who had close-cropped hair and designer sunglasses. The harbourmaster was behind a pane of glass, mouthing like a goldfish.

He poked his head above the glass and leered. "GOT SOMETHING SPECIAL FOR YOU," he called above the stubbled heads. In the hush

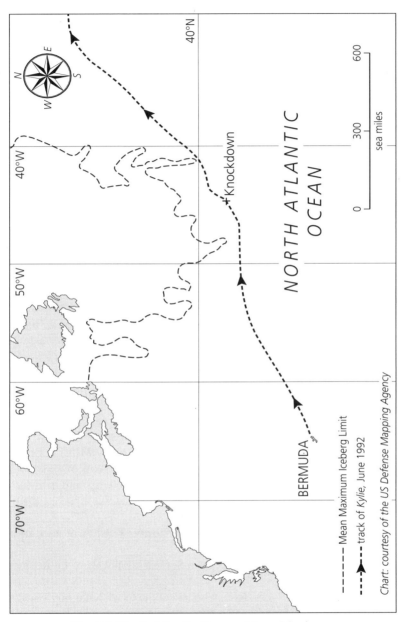

Chart 8: North Atlantic Ocean : Mean Maximum
Ice Limit, June 1988.

that followed, pairs of dark glasses followed the passage of a fat envelope as it was handed backwards.

"A liddle present from your homelandt, I think?" said one.

As always with a person in dark glasses, his expression was inscrutable.

"It can't be; it's got no stamps on."

"But it says 'Priority' and 'Urgent', so it must be important, yes?" he said, holding the envelope to his ear and squeezing it. "Gaskets for the motor, I think."

"But I haven't got a motor."

"Ho-ho! You make a joke."

In the envelope was a two-page communication from COMIN-TICEPAT, said by me as *Comintissáypat* to go with Eliot's "peculiar, and more dignified" cat-names such as Quaxo or Coricopat, and had then passed between other bodies with even odder, but no less impressive, names such as NAVOCEANCOMFAC and COMSUB-LANT until it had got to St George's, where someone had written MR HANCOCK – PRIORITY on an envelope and put the message in it.

Not counting the intervening giants in dark glasses, I worked out that the message had come to me sixth-hand. Looking at the names listed at the head of it, I felt as if I were about to read a chain letter asking me to send ten pounds to the above-named on the promise that I would receive a million pounds by return of post. The penalty for breaking the chain was an outbreak of dire misfortune, followed by a lingering and painful death.

In fact, when I had squeezed out of the office and could read it without being overlooked, the message asked all ships between 40N and 52N, 39W and 57W to report ice-sightings to COMINTICEPAT every six hours, and then went on to give the whereabouts of all known ice, which, on 31st May 1992, included many icebergs and growlers north of 42° 30'N, and an object described as "an isolated radar target" forty-four miles to the south.

I liked getting a messsage labelled "Priority" but felt in need of a glossary to go with it.

"What do they mean by a 'target'? Something put there by Reagan for his Star Wars?"

"Don't be absurd," said José, who had come to wish me *bon voyage* bearing a bottle of brandy and a five-day-old copy of *The Times*; "it's a hadbag discarded by Lady T."

"'Sprobably a growler," said the harbourmaster, who had come out of his office to see off the giants. "Sometimes they get as far south as Bermuda before they melt."

When José had gone back to his seventy-footer I worked out that by the time *Kylie* got to 42° 30'N the ice bulletin would be twelve days old. Which way would the ice have drifted by then, and at what rate? I scribbled figures, plotted positions and pencilled in a line which seemed, after the brandy, to enclose an area not much smaller than the red hand of 1988, with the same knuckle lying across the Admiralty route and a small fat finger poking south of the fortieth parallel.

I awarded myself half a spoonful of marmalade and a pipe of St Bruno. If *Kylie* had enough people aboard for someone to be on watch all the time, crossing the ice area would be acceptable, but in my crewless state I didn't think I'd be able to stay awake long enough to keep a constant lookout. To dog-leg south of the ice-fingers would add a hundred miles to the passage, but, in terms of peace of mind, the extra distance would be worth it.

On the morning of 1st June José followed *Kylie* out of harbour in a rigid inflatable, taking photos as she passed through Town Cut. Off Mills Breaker buoy he motored alongside and handed me the camera. I passed him a slip of paper with a Southwold phone number written on it. "And whatever else you do," I shouted above the loud gurgles from the engine, "don't call her till the end of July because she still thinks that you're aboard as crew."

I latched-in the wind vane, set up the preventer, poled out the genoa to a fifteen-knot south-west wind and headed for the first waypoint, 515 miles distant. All about me a brilliant blue sea was pressing eastwards, trailing small runners of fine white lace. I sat on a cushion on the coachroof with my back to the mast, feeling happy and excited at the prospect of making the crossing alone. Far from letting me down, José Lamas had sent me off from Bermuda on a wonderful upswing. Sartre says somewhere that in spite of friendhip, couplings on the marriage-bed or prayers to deities, Man remains always alone; that, however hard he tries, he cannot communicate to anyone else the innermost core of his feelings. It is an opinion well worth half a pint of bitter beer to argue over. More to the point so far as I was concerned is the fact that, however poorly we tell of the experience, from time to time our spirit does indeed feel at one with some other. The sensation may be as fleeting as winter sunshine, but we know it. And sitting on *Kylie*'s foredeck, setting out from Bermuda on the passage home, I felt a oneness with Pip that would not have been possible if another person had been there with me.

29

Christie

Through a long jagged tear in the clouds I could see a lot of Leo but didn't know for certain if I was looking at Denebola, or if Rasalhague lay to the west or the east. Not so long ago there had been a time when I could have recognised these stars, but since then I had bought myself the satellite navigator, which – no doubt about it – was taking over my brain. Stars out or not, so long as the battery kept its amps, at every moment of the passage these bright green figures on the grey screen down here in the cabin could be telling me where I was. Every time I looked at them, however, my brain forgot a little bit more about the heavens. Drinking José's brandy at the end of the graveyard watch, I stared into the screen with a slow-burning fascination which sputtered from time to time with doubts. Dimly in the background I could see a row of shadowy figure 8s. It seemed that every letter and figure on display had been formed from an 8. I found this disturbing, but also, in some ways, strangely beautiful. It could very well be, I thought, that the figure 8 was an archetypal mother giving birth to shining children who knew a brief moment of brilliant glory and then died and went back into her body. The idea was thrilling stuff, on a par with learning about the *Girl Pat*. But, by leaning just a little farther sideways and going on sipping brandy, it became obvious that the arithmetic which the satnav was practising was nowhere near as soundly based as its background philosophy. From the way in which the shining figures were being arrived at, it seemed that the satnav was getting its 9s by subtracting 1 from 8. I sippped a little more brandy and tutted. No good would come of these goings-on if the basic rules of arithmetic were being flouted.

The genoa sheet clattered. I hushed it, poured another brandy and pressed a button. On the misty screen appeared six fat ladies queueing for a bus.

I had to admit that, however wrongly it got them, the satnav's figures had kept me clear of quite a few dangers when the stars themselves had been invisible. Because of the satnav, I had been able to close a lee shore of Yucatán with the certain knowledge that I was heading for a channel which led to shelter.

But, again, modern technology was taking away a deal of pleasure from passage-making as I had once known it, when the ship's day and my astro-biological clock had run from one meridian altitude of the sun to the next, the excitement coming to a climax with the ruling-off of the figures in the workbook and the plotting of *Kylie*'s position on the chart at noon. I still started the ship's day at noon, but now the sun had been made redundant it would have been more practical to start it at midnight when I opened a new page in the log. All in all, I thought, the satnav was so easy to use that it smacked of the devil. The pencil addings-up and taking-aways which led up to the plotting of the noon position had been done away with and the sextant had fallen out of use; soon it would be antique. The depressing thing was, without even looking once at the stars I might very well circle the world. Crossing from the Canaries to the West Indies only three years previously, the sextant had been in and out of its wooden box almost every day, but since the little grey plastic box with the satnav had been screwed on to the coaming above the chart table I had taken the sun's altitude half a dozen times at most. The satnav had done me out of a job; it wouldn't do. I told myself I would drink a beer, switch off the satnav and take a sun-sight. The trouble was, the sextant having been stowed behind a fiddle-bar above the starboard midships locker and wedged in by a couple of Le Carré novels and out-of-date distress flares, taking a sight would need an awful lot of preparation. Also, holding it up to my eye for minutes at a time made my arm ache. But I would get it out tomorrow, definitely . . .

At eleven the next morning I rolling-hitched a lanyard from my safety harness to the latch of the steering gear. Now, if I dozed off and fell overboard before taking the sun-sight, my bodyweight would yank the latch and *Kylie* would come into the wind and stop dead. Having set things to my satisfaction, I went to the cabin for a beer. I woke at half-past twelve, the unopened can beside me and the sun past its zenith. Two weeks were to pass before I had another go at getting the sextant out of its case.

I drank up the beer and cooked an early dinner of cauliflower cheese. While waiting for the pressure cooker to raise a head of steam I put on a pair of earphones the size of small soup-plates and turned the dial of the Brookes and Gatehouse radio-receiver, another piece of splendid vintage equipment which was falling into disuse. The last time I had uncoiled the direction-finding attachment had been years ago, in the middle of the North Sea, when it had picked up the Isle of May beacon as clear as a bell at 130 miles. Now, through the earphones came a programme of pop music from Radio Bermuda, also 130 miles distant but sounding rather tinny. Still with the earphones on, I was sprinkling my dinner with Worcester sauce when the singing stopped abruptly and a voice said that Hurricane Christie was centred 350 miles south-east of Bermuda, was moving 345 degrees at fifteen knots, bringing wind speeds of 90 knots, and that the island's services were on Red Alert.

I ate only two forkfuls of cauliflower cheese. I felt like biting my thumb. Twenty-four hours at fifteen knots would put the hurricane right on top of me.

I scraped cauliflower cheese overboard and tapped the barometer: 1021 mbs and rising. The satnav said that *Kylie* was making 5.5 knots in what was no more than a light-to-moderate southerly wind. The sky was three-eighths cloud but was looking nothing out of the ordinary. I stood facing the wave crests, raised my right arm to shoulder height in line with my body and pressed it backwards forty-five degrees, as though in the first stage of a chest-development course of the sort which used to feature a Rudyard Kipling figure with bent arrows whizzing round his limbs. According to a meteorological law made up by a Dutchman, the low pressure lay to the north-west, in the direction of my wagging arm, dead opposite to the track of up-and-coming Christie.

A sail appeared, far to the south and heading – so far as I could make out through the binoculars – into the path of the hurricane.

"Sailboat heading east, this is *Kylie*."

Ten seconds of silence. I take the walkie-talkie up to the coachroof and say it again with the battery turned up to full power.

"Any station. Any station. This is *Kylie* . . . *Kylie*."

Thirty seconds go by. I put down the walkie-talkie on the cockpit duckboard and gaze at the compass. Had I got my figures wrong? I am steering 080°, so sixteen degrees of westerly error means that the true course is 064°, doesn't it? And a hurricane coming at me from the south-east will be tracking about north-west and will possibly curve to the north or even north-east, right?

I see the other sail is still heading east. Damn him! Whatever he was doing, I ought to be heading south-west, out of the path of the storm.

I gybe onto port tack, head west and note the change of course in the log.

Twenty minutes later, on the hour, the pop music stops again and Radio Bermuda reminds its listeners that Hurricane Christie is a fictional creation, part of a training exercise.

30

Down for the Third Time

Kylie sailed 248 miles in two days before the south-westerly faltered and gave way to easterly airs. In the next two days she sailed only 90 miles, not many of them in the direction in which I wanted to go: the bows sometimes pointing towards Greenland and, at others, the Sahara Desert, hardly ever towards the waypoint. Genoa down, ghoster up; ghoster down, spinnaker up; spinnaker down, nothing up. Tired by the sail-changes, in the middle of the third day I took to my berth, set the alarm clock to go off in two hours and tucked it under my chin. When I woke the deckhead was gleaming redly in the sunset. I had slept for six.

Mares' tails crept in from the north-west, some of them fifty miles long. "Strong wind coming soon," I thought; but at midday on day five the wind was still light-to-moderate, although it had veered a point south, so letting me steer nearer the course and make good 112 miles in 24 hours. I scrubbed the cockpit teak. That afternoon the wind blew from a smeary grey sky and the barometer slowly fell. In spite of these warnings *Kylie* carried the large genoa throughout the night, most of which I spent below in my berth. By slow degrees the wind veered south-east and then south, until by the end of the sixth day it was blowing from west of south and I was able to ease the sheets and steer for the waypoint.

I tried to keep up with news of home. *The Times*, now 12 days old, reported that 25th May 1992 had been the hottest Spring Bank Holiday on record. In London the Conservative party had had a grand beano to celebrate Mr Major's election victory. Far to the west in Swansea, a boy and girl had been taken to hospital after falling fifteen feet when a railing collapsed under them while they were kissing.

I took up half a turn on the backstays, shortened the clew outhaul pendant, removed rust stains from deck eyeplates and bound a chafe-guard to the starboard upper guardrail.

On the following day, the wind still moderate from the south-west,

I re-spliced the tack tackle of the foresails, greased the bow-roller and de-rusted tools.

A sail came in sight at west-north-west. I twiddled the squelcher of the walkie-talkie, cleared my throat and waited.

"This is *Schedar*. Camden, Maine, to the Azores."

"*Kylie*. Bermuda for Ireland. Peter Hancock."

"Say that again. Is that right . . .? Peter Hancock . . .?"

"Yes . . . yes. I mean . . . er . . . Roger."

"Ha! My name is Haddock . . . Peter Haddock."

We laughed loudly but uneasily, as though we had come across each other wearing the same overcoats. According to his short-wave radio a weather front was approaching from Newfoundland, bringing with it a south-west gale.

I watched *Schedar* pass to the south. I hoped the gale would come sooner rather than later, while *Kylie* still had a good offing from the ice.

By the end of the seventh day I had sailed 660 miles and was 270 from a crucial waypoint south of the ice, the weather was still fair, the wind SW ten knots, but the barometer was slowly falling. On the eighth day, with the wind at 25 knots and *Kylie* heading east by north, I ate the last banana and wondered about the true whereabouts of the ice. Was my fifteen-mile-a-day estimate of its rate of drift quite enough? If it wasn't, a berg might be waiting for me at the waypoint. I shifted the waypoint farther south, bit into what looked like a Granny Smith apple but turned out to be something much softer, altered course ten degrees to starboard and changed the small genoa for the working jib, bruising my right foot against the cleat as I lurched across the foredeck. Half an hour later I wrenched my right elbow while reefing the mainsail.

The seas became higher, their crests thwacking against the hull and filling the cockpit about once an hour and – in spite of the storm boards – sometimes spattering the galley. Even so, the going was good, with *Kylie* careering through tumbling crests and the bow wave curving upwards as high as the lower guardrail. At ten that night, with a strong wind and moderate seas on the starboard beam, the boat was wearing a deeply reefed mainsail and a small jib. Lit by a wan moon, the waves came at me sideways, their crests peaking higher as they ran into the tumbling surge from *Kylie*'s bows. I watched them from the weather side of the cockpit, my left hand on the tiller, right arm crooked round a winch and left seaboot braced against the opposite sidebench.

187

By morning it was blowing a small gale from the south and the sea was blue marble veined white, the crests dribbling down its hollow cheeks. I clipped on a second safety line. *Kylie* skittered across the slopes, her jibsail like pressed steel.

At sunset I was ten miles south of the crucial waypoint, the waves running fifteen feet and me feeling I could not steer for very much longer. Above the lurching masthead, clouds were scudding in opposite directions.

Sometime after midnight the wind fell to force 6. I latched in the vane, cooked a corned-beef hash, and smoked my first pipe in twelve hours. In spite of the fact that the cockpit duckboard was still occasionally floating, that I was pumping forty strokes an hour and was having difficulty making tea, the barometer was insisting that the weather was getting better by the hour.

Before dawn came the stronger wind returned with a series of gusty broadsides and blew a whole gale. After two days of it I altered course thirty degrees north and wrote in the log "Must be past the ice fingertip by now".

The course alteration made the boat's motion less violent, bringing the south-south-west wind from squarely abeam to the starboard quarter and taking the edge off its strength.

An awkward cross-swell set in from the west. Till then the swell had been running true to the wind but now it was coming sixty degrees to the seas, making them higher and steeper, and their breakers less predictable. The windspeed increased to about 45 knots, strong enough to lean on. I didn't lean on it for long. The idea of *Kylie* being caught sideways on by 25-ft waves, described by Beaufort as "High, with tumbling crests", made the threat of icebergs looming up to leeward seem trivial. I took down the storm jib and streamed a hundred miles of rope. At 38°N, 45°W, eleven hundred miles from Bermuda, *Kylie* turned her back to the gale and ran before it with no sail up. Apart from pumping the bilge and counting the teaspoons, there seemed little else to be done. Though mentioned by Beaufort, the possibility of chimneypots falling about one's ears seemed remote. Lying-to was out of the question: the seas were the wrong shape and too big. *Kylie* had got past the ice finger but was now running straight for the knuckle.

There came lull, and heavy breakers got noticeably fewer. Sure that the wind vane could cope, at half-past four one afternoon I pulled down the hinged flap, lifted the upper washboards out of their channel and squeezed through the companion hatch into the cabin to snatch a fifty-minute sleep on the sole between the berths. At ten minutes to five my body rose to the underside of the coachroof and stayed there. *The Complete Works of Shakespeare* flew across the cabin, pursued by four oranges. There was a loud roar.

Kylie had suffered her third knockdown.

31

Shark in Aspic

To a medley of clatters, nineteen rice puddings, seven corned beefs, four tomato soups and a nameless rabble of other canned foods were jolted around beneath the berths as *Kylie* levered herself briskly upright. As always when hard pressed, she treated me more gently. Like a nicely done egg on its way from the frying pan to the plate, I was jiggled across the lining of the coachroof and eased down its curved sides until I could be laid unbroken but quivering on the cabin sole with my sunny side up. Spluttering through her washboards, the boat lurched sidelong again, dashing the kettle against the raised lip of the chart table. Water dribbled from its spout onto my face.

I stowed the kettle in the galley locker, slid back the bolt on the upper washboard and looked astern. The steering gear was still in place on the rudder head, its vane cocked alertly, and though the compass had turned turtle it was still in its bracket. So far as I could see from the hatchway the only signs that anything out of the ordinary had taken place were the torrents of water cascading off the side-decks and the josh of water in the half-filled cockpit.

A breaker the size of a single-decker bus roared towards the starboard quarter, slewed sideways at the last moment and broke in a welter of foam. I put my hand out of the cabin and clipped on a safety line. Before *Kylie* could slide into the trough I had scrambled into the cockpit and rammed fast the washboard behind me. I clipped a second line to the harness and went on inspecting the deck gear. My first thought was for the dinghy.

When it is pumped up ready to be rowed, the dinghy resembles in shape a seven-foot doughnut, but before setting off on sea passages I squeeze the air out of it and truss it down tightly on the coachroof. With a two-gallon water-container and packages of rations and distress flares rolled within, the dinghy then looks like a large snake digesting a small arthritic camel.

But the coachroof was bare. The knockdown had torn the dinghy from its lashings; now it was flapping above my head, its hindquarters straddling the boom and its foreparts clinging to the mast, trembling like a half-drowned pup. It took me half an hour to coax it back to the coachroof and ten minutes more to fasten it down in its proper place.

Seventy-two strokes on the pump had sucked the bilge empty and I was feeling an urge to brew a pint of tea. Before I could get below to fill the kettle another cubic yard of salt water dumped itself into the cockpit. Rather than make tea, I thought I had better steer *Kylie* for a while.

Rushing along at an angle which plunged deeply into and slightly across the seas was like going down a slope of grass and scree among the mountains of Snowdonia, the general lie of the gradient clear, but the going underfoot slippery and uncertain, and Tryfan or Glyder Fach always in the corner of the eye, their summits looming above me like the waves. One difference between the peaks of mountains and those of high seas however, is that in the open ocean the crests between the observer and the sun sometimes become transparent in a way that mountain tops never do unless they are capped with ice. Now, half an hour before the sun set on the North Atlantic, when a high sea ran against a swell and peaked an instant before breaking, the sun shone directly through the crests and bathed the opposite cliffs of ocean with lurid light. The slant of the beams made the troughs of the waves seem more like caverns than they really were, and when, from time to time, the sun was hidden by cloud, the scene became grim. I hooded my head more tightly at these moments, for it seemed to me as if the wind gods were digging vast oceanic trenches to receive the victims of the holocaust which *The Times* said was about to be enacted in Bosnia. But the terrible scene was touched with beauty too, for now and then the wave tops briefly gleamed turquoise, and sometimes the crests were filled with delicate orange beams as they tumbled to leeward. With my hooded eyes for most of the time on the dangers coming from astern, I wove east-north-eastwards, gripping the tiller. Then, plunging down into an cavern which was deeper and darker than any others, I lifted my eyes to the watery peak on the far side of it. *Kylie* sank into deep shadow, the sunlight shone briefly golden through a wavecrest, and in it was a huge black fish. I wondered what to make of it.

Although my great-aunt Florrie usually told fortunes only when she was gazing into well-drained tea cups, she was quite good at reading the future from haphazard happenings too, such as when, on seeing me drop a spent match into the porridge pan on a morning on which I thought the only adventure in store was a visit to Uzzell's sweet shop, she straightaway said that I was about to go on a very long journey. Sure enough, soon after she had said this I found myself whirling towards Colwyn Bay on an LMS train with my bucket and spade. Now, fifty-four years later, I would have liked to have heard her foretell what the future held for a great-nephew who had just seen a shark embalmed in aspic.

An hour or so after my sighting the shark the heavy westerly swell went down and the wind fell away to twenty-five knots, which let me put the kettle on at last and make the course for Ireland. While running before the gale *Kylie* had been heading straight for the ice knuckle eighty miles to the north, but now I had re-set the steering gear the boat was edging safely away from it. I brewed a potful of extra-strong tea and lay down on the cabin sole, knowing that, with the wind and swell at last easing, I had a good chance of staying there long enough to finish my nap.

At dawn the wind was down to only a whisper beneath a drizzling sky the colour of dirty dishcloths. Before long the drizzle had turned into a steady downpour. I stuffed rags into the scuppers and baled six gallons of rainwater from the side-decks into the water cans, after which I lashed the duckboard to a stanchion and gave myself a bath in the cockpit. *Kylie* nuzzled across a light ESE wind, making four knots through rain which sheeted down without a break for thirty hours, by which time the scene had taken on the tedious languor of an epic by de Mille. Peering out at it, I should not have been surprised to see a bargeload of disgruntled Mayan extras looming up out of the rain and a bald head poking down through the clouds to cry "ACTION!" The downpour made life much less agreeable than it normally was, for the gale had gone through all my changes of dry clothing, and although during the first hour of the downpour I had laundered three pairs of cotton shorts, two of trousers, four terylene shirts and a couple of acrylic pullovers, I was down to my last pair of dry longjohns and a moth-eaten but very warm lambswool jersey which, in spite of a forbidding sniff from Nigel, Terrie and I had plucked from a dustbin in Maine. Because of this, after doing the laundry I spent the day below deck, putting only my head and shoulders out into the streaming cockpit every twenty minutes or so to make sure that I was not about to be run down by a colossal tanker. Visibility was two miles at the most. For the first and what I hope will be the last time in my travels I began to feel forlorn. As day merged with night and the rain went on without a pause, the feeling deepened into one of rejection which even the playing of the *Pastoral Symphony* could not dispel.

I put my head into the Brookes and Gatehouse in an effort to hear not only the time signal from station WWV but also the worldwide reports of cyclonic disturbances which followed it at eight and ten minutes past the hour. In spite of salvoes of crackles and hisses I heard the long peep of the time signal clearly, and then a synthesised voice began to tell of the gales. I held my pencil at the ready but hardly used it because I could make out only one word in ten. The voice was scarcely different in tone from the one which urges Underground travellers to Mind The Gap, but in this case the syllables came through my headphones no more clearly than the tolling of a church bell with a muffled clapper. After listening to a hundred distorted words which were supposed to be informing me about storms and their likely paths I had written only "110 knots". A wind of 110 knots? But in which part of the ocean was it blowing? I rolled the pencil between my palms and sweated. "Mind the gap" was right; hearing bits and pieces of news was worse than hearing no news at all. Knowing nothing is a safer state to be in than knowing any number of unconnected somethings when you can't bridge the gaps. I shone the flashlight into a plastic mug and peered at the tea leaves.

The next bulletin from WWV came through the headphones at full volume but left me none the wiser. After half a minute of failing to make out whether the first storm in the list was tracking across the North Pacific Ocean or the North Atlantic, I coiled up the earphones and pulled the plug. It seemed that until I had got into earshot of whichever of the BBC's home-service programmes could be picked up by the little pocket-radio in its rack next to the oil lamp, any forecasts of oncoming storms would have to come over the walkie-talkie from nearby ships, if and when I saw them.

The rain petered out during the morning of the sixteenth day but the sky stayed heavily overcast, and the wind remained light from an easterly quarter. I pottered about in the gloomy cockpit, stringing sodden shirts to the weather guardrail, oiling the log clock and peering into the steel-grey ocean in the hope of seeing dolphins. Only a few years before, from the Bay of Biscay onwards during the passage to the Mediterranean, and later, during the crossing from the Canary Islands to the West Indies, hardly a day had gone by without seeing flying fishes whirring across the sea or schools of dolphins, some of them hundreds strong, leaping out of the waves. Their bustling activity had delighted the eye and excited the mind, and I was missing them keenly. Apart from the shark, since leaving Bermuda on this eastbound crossing I had seen no fish of any kind, and only a couple or so of birds.

Nor much of the sun neither. Not seeing it for several days together did not at all hinder navigation during this middle part of the passage, for now that *Kylie* was clear of the ice it did not matter much if the Dead Reckoning position which I pencilled on the chart at midday every day was ten or twenty miles different from where I truly was. The problem was that the further north I went the more necessary was it for *Kylie* to be sailing in long spells of sunshine so that the solar panels could replenish her battery. When fully charged the battery had contained 90 amp-hours of electricity. If I switched on a neon-tube cabin light for, say, two hours every night, the chart light for one hour and the masthead tricolour lantern for six hours I would use up 18 amps every twenty-four hours. To put back the same number of amps into the battery, the solar panels needed to be in direct sunlight and as near as possible at a right angle to the rays for six hours a day. Until the skies clouded over three days before the gale came, the battery had been getting enough amps to live on. Then, *Kylie* had been mostly running free on the port tack with the panels tilted towards the sun so that her electrical income had exceeded her expenditure by a small amount. The result, as Micawber would have said, was happiness. But now, after nine days under cloudy skies and tilted away from the sun on the starboard tack, the solar panels had re-charged the battery hardly at all and I was feeling prickles of anxiety. So as to keep enough charge in it to power the navigation light and the satnav during the final five hundred miles of the passage, on the evening of the sixteenth day I cut down the use of the neon lights in the cabin to under an hour and – a bigger saving by far – sailed through the night with the navigation light switched off.

On the seventeenth day, still under grey skies and with no prospect of a sun-sight, I ran the satnav for half an hour and found I was more than half way between Bermuda and Fastnet, making a speed of what the instrument claimed was 6.7 knots while in the process of getting its bearings but only 4.5 knots by the time it had sorted through them and was recording "POOR FIX". The wind then blew at twenty-five knots from the south-east, so I went to the mast to take in a second reef. In the course of doing it a sail car jammed in the track a couple of feet above my reach. I climbed up to it by putting my right foot on the mast winch and my left on the boom. By tapping against the track with the winch handle and gently twisting the eye of the car with a small spike, I managed to free it. Before I could climb back down on to the deck and finish putting in the reef, the boat lurched to windward and I fell, striking my right elbow on the winch on the way to the deck.

It was not a heavy blow; most of the pain had gone by the time I had made up the halyard and clambered back to the cockpit, and what was left of it went away as soon as I had swallowed the last of José's five-star brandy. I thought at the time that I had got off scot free, without even a bruise or a swelling to remind me, but later that afternoon I went out into the cockpit to look at the horizon and shortly after doing so I changed my mind.

The wind had gone down, and *Kylie* was reaching across a grey sea with the same heavy sullen cloud above. A long low swell was coming from the south, raising false horizons. To weather, there were no ships to be seen, no birds and no fish. I disentangled a pair of sodden trousers from the rigging, tossed them down into the cabin and looked to leeward. Swimming alongside was a dolphin.

The creature was about six feet long, its back a clerical grey and its sides patterned lengthways with a pair of narrow black stripes. It slid through the water two or three feet below the surface, keeping in step with the boat and coming up to breathe about once a minute. Very glad of its company, I leant outboard to peer at it more closely and to relish the kinship of a fellow creature which had warm blood. There was no more than six feet of air and water between us, and every now and then the dolphin tilted sideways until its nearer eye was looking directly at me. The iris was dark mahogany in colour, and to the rear of the eye, between the slate-grey back and the first of the elegant side-stripes, was an unexpected blaze of yellow. The dash of bright colour gave the creature a raffish air, like a sporty handkerchief does in the breast pocket of a suit. The dolphin could have been impersonating a bank clerk sloping off for an afternoon at the races.

The dolphin came up for air and I tried to call a cheerful greeting to it, but all that came out was a croak. I gargled a quantity of salt water in the hope of flushing my tubes, put a smile on my face and tried again. "Hello!" I called once more to the dolphin, but in spite of the smile the greeting came out sounding no more cheerful than before. I don't know how such a thing could happen, but it seemed that the blow to the elbow had gone to my throat.

From that day to this my voice has never got back to how it used to be.

At 44$^{1}/_{2}$ °N, 38°W I saw from the chart that although *Kylie* was well past halfway across the Atlantic she was still three hundred miles miles nearer to Nova Scotia than to Scotland. The discovery appalled me. I thought I had left the New World far behind weeks ago, but here it still was, dogging my track like a hungry wolf. Far from its being an aid to navigation, Mercator's distorted projection was nothing but a web of false promises. Thinking this, I turned my back on the chart table for an hour and made and ate half a dozen tortillas.

On the 20th day I pored over the logbook and noted that for eight days in a row the wind had been blowing from the south-east, although all this time I had recorded that the clouds had been travelling against it from the west. How could this be? Perhaps the blow to the elbow had damaged not only my larynx but my brain . . .? I held to a north-easterly course towards where I supposed the westerlies would be blowing, and looked for guidance to *The Times*. Although by this time its weather page was long out of date, its astronomer informed me that between the 22nd and 26th of June I could observe Mercury pass below Castor and Pollux in Gemini until they formed an almost a straight line. On the other hand, whether the sky cleared and I saw this happen or not, I learnt from another column that, even if I wanted to do so, I should be unable to sit in on the 188th Annual General Meeting of the British and Foreign Bible Society because it had been held in London on the 19th.

At 19h 03m on the day of the Summer Solstice I stood still under the sun and turned over a small tinful of Bermudan coins. It was a quiet evening, with the wind at SE, moderate, and at last after twelve days the cloud had thinned. The sun was as if a torch shining through the walls of a tent, allowing me just enough light in which to read an eye-destroying text of *As You Like It* in the lee of the sprayhood.

A tanker overtook me on passage from Corpus Christi to Sullum Voe. From it I learnt that the forecast was for headwinds, but for fifteen hours afterwards the wind stayed west of south and pushed me a further 70 miles nearer Ireland.

Knowing from the course of the tanker that I was now on a shipping route, I switched on the tricolour lantern and left it on throughout the night. At seven the following morning, under a yellowy-grey sky and with the sea again looking like polished steel, I got out my smallest sail needle and sat at the foot of the mast, herringboning a nine-inch vertical tear in the luff of the mainsail which had got there through my not taking a sail-car through the gate of the track when I had last reefed sail. Between three and four in the dismal afternoon, picking through the mixture of stores hanging in netting-bags above the berths, I found that a cabbage from Bermuda had stayed unmouldy for fifeeen days, and that packaged bread was still eatable eighteen days after purchase if the mould was cut off before spreading it with thick-cut marmalade. I noted down these discoveries in large bold letters.

By now the battery was so very low that the satnav was not working, and so it seemed certain that I would have to use the sextant if and when I saw the sun again. I unwound a skein of coarse saffron weed from the rotator and re-set the log, and then lay hove-to for half an hour to drill out and replace a sheared bolt on the steering gear.

These events too I noted, but in much smaller writing than before.

32
Sailing Home

"For whatever we lose (like a you or a me)
it's always ourselves we find in the sea"

e. e. cummings

Six hundred miles west of Fastnet the cabin was filled with the sound of racquets hitting balls at Wimbledon, then the voice of a BBC weather forecaster saying that a high of 1026 millibars off Finisterre would decline to 1022. A passing ship to which I eventually spoke added that a low of 998 was developing south-west of me.

There followed a night and day with *Kylie* rising and falling to a high swell from the south-east and another bout of heavy continuous rain.

The swell became higher, forty feet from trough to crest, and continued for three days. No ships, no dolphins, no birds. I felt that the world was in the throes of tremendous apocalyptic convulsions and I was the only creature to survive them. I pictured myself cast up on a barren smoking volcano sans teeth, sans eyes, sans everything. I knelt on the cabin sole, screwed up my eyes and asked that I should not go altogether mad; then, feeling a little better for saying my thoughts, nibbled a pecan biscuit and worked out the approximate noon altitude of the sun in the faint hope of glimpsing it.

At 1130 on day 27 I saw it for the first time in more than a week. In spite of a fuzzy horizon, I snatched three sights of its lower limb, used the mean of the altitudes and times, and from these went on to work out and lay off a position line. In the afternoon I glimpsed the lower limb again and laid off a second position line. From their crossing, it seemed that Fastnet was bearing 099° by 302 miles and that *Kylie* was making good 5 knots on a course which was no better than 035°.

By this time the sun had disappeared in fog. Every two minutes or so I blew on the conch shell I had brought from Paradise, but after half an hour of it I gave up and made a batch of pancakes. I was eating the last of them when two pigeons flew out of the fog. They circled the boat three times before landing on the dinghy.

At seven, in a light south-easterly I put about on to port tack and stayed on it till two in the morning, all the time without a navigation light, and then backed the foresail and lay hove-to and slept till twenty-past five, leaving the pigeons side by side in the cockpit.

"Aha!" I croaked when I woke. "You've lost your way, haven't you? You don't navigate by a cerebral compass at all, do you?"

Tired, bedraggled, cold, they paddled their pink feet on the dinghy, and so I spread out the centre page of *The Times* and invited them into the cabin. After a meal of brown rice, they drank a little water, fluffed out their feathers and settled down. As in my own relationship, the male partner chose the side nearest to the light-switch.

"You got yourselves lost, right?" I said to them before going back to the cockpit. "And why was that, I wonder? Was it because a packet of iron filings between your ears got all shook up? Of *course* not. You're not carrying compasses at all, are you? Admit it: *you lost your way because you couldn't see the sun.*"

With her soiled feathers and scraggy neck, the hen bird was not at all beautiful but she was the more confident of the two, letting me stroke her at will and clucking her approval at the quality of the rice. I named her Iseult, and her mate Tristram.

The names did not fit the circumstance but because they were the first names I had thought of, they would have to do. *Kylie* and her white sail would replace the black sail of death in the ancient legend; these modern lovers would not die. The passage would end well for them and for me: of that I was sure.

My kindliness lasted eight hours. At dawn the following morning I opened up the cabin and, holding my nose, recoiled straightaway into the cockpit. Pigeons, I tell you, excrete more than they ingest.

Our relationships quickly reached breaking point. Iseult turned out to be a pouting hussy who ignored house rules. Having watched me clean up the cabin and heard my firm command to stay in the cockpit, she blinked her orange eyes, clicked her beak and fluttered onto the chart table. Her feet paddled among the Azores.

I shooed her back to the cockpit and put a saucerful of rice at convenient pecking height; seconds later she hooked the saucer onto the duckboard. "Bad girl!" I said hoarsely. I spread the back page of *The Times* on the duckboard and said "Number twos on that, if you please, and nowhere else." She immediately scuttled over to her mate and instructed him to relieve himself on the compass.

"Anarchist!" I croaked, wiping runny green deposits from the lubber's line. Iseult flounced back onto the chart table and stood on Greenland.

I took hold of Tristram and gave him a talking-to about the necessity for ship's discipline. By the end of it he was pretending to be bored.

"Listen, stupid," I said, shaking him; "the fog's gone! That round thing above your head is called the sun; now just you take a bearing of it and go home."

I hurled him aloft. He circled the boat once and headed east-north-east.

Iseult crouched low, a dowdy huddle of feathers. For some reason she was trembling.

"Stop trying it on," I said. "Don't you try to get round me, my girl; I know your sort."

I threw her upwards. She beat her wings very much faster than her mate had done. Like applause in a television panel-game, the clatter seemed overdone; and it didn't help to keep her going upwards. From a starting height of twenty feet, in two seconds she was down to ten feet and in three her wings were pounding the sea and her unblinking orange eyes were staring into mine.

I grabbed onto a backstay and reached out towards her.

Until that moment, casual observation had led me to take it for granted that birds are not programmed to beat one wing independently of the other. But that was exactly what happened: the pigeon beat her right wing on the water and, at the same time, stretched out her left one towards me until it was fully extended and rigid. But the yard of space between her wing-tip and my outstretched hand was too great for us to bridge, and soon her waterlogged feathers had dragged her down until only her head, upper back and wings were above the suface.

"Come on, little one!" I cried. "Come *on!*"

She angled her wing-beats so that they propelled as well as supported, and the orange eyes fixed on my outstretched fingers. The brain behind those eyes was smaller than a peanut, and the body was as crushable as a paper bag, yet Iseult had a strength of will greater perhaps than my own.

My fingers stretched inches further too, and the pigeon's wing seemed to get longer. The wing beat on the water and her body floundered across the yard of sea between us. I gripped the wingtip between thumb and finger and plucked her into the cockpit. Inches behind me, a woman was sobbing.

Two hours later I finished drying the feathers. The fog had come back, and my voice was saying "The way I see it, you were in a race from Southampton to Merthyr Tydfil and he was on another from, say, Birmingham to Barnstaple. Above the Bristol Channel your tracks crossed, and before anyone could say 'Barbara Cartland' you'd eloped. Have some more rice and . . . Listen, I'm sorry about the oil on your neck – it's the fault of those tankers pumping out their sludge on the way to Sullum Voe."

She trudged to a corner of the cockpit and turned her back on me.

"Come on," I said, "it's no use moping. He left four hours ago, and now that the fog's come down again he can't find his way back to where we are so he's done the sensible thing and booked into a bed-and-breakfast till the weather clears."

Iseult shook her head and closed her eyes. I left her to her misery and went below, thinking that, likely as not, Tristram was already billing and cooing at a plumper hen somewhere this side of Skibbereen.

"Come on, little one!"

Well, when the wind came again we would be less than 300 miles from Baltimore, and there'd be enough cock pigeons in County Cork for her to find a new mate . . . If she got over her misery, that was.

I lit a pipe and opened the chart of Ireland.

It would be an awful thing if she were to peg out now, after all the suffering she'd been through.

"Keep your pecker up," I called, glancing out to the cockpit. I need not have worried. Alongside her was another, larger pigeon. Unmistakably, it was Tristram. How he had found his way back to *Kylie* through a blanket of fog after flying four-and-a-half hours, perhaps as much as a hundred miles towards Ireland before turning back again, I do not begin to know.

A hundred miles from Fastnet the breeze backed west and fell away. *Kylie* wallowed about in a mixture of swells. I carried an anchor on deck, prised out the plug of the navel pipe and shackled on the cable. At half past one in the afternoon I at last got a fix which put me eight miles ahead of my Dead Reckoning and ninety miles from Fastnet. That evening, noticing that the compass had been excreted on, I lifted the pigeons from the sidebenches and put them yet again on the duckboard,

On the second of July it blew south-south-east force 7 and *Kylie* lay hove-to, her bows pointing westward, the birds huddled in the lee of the cockpit coaming and myself below deck in a quagmire of fatigue. I came to at six-thirty and saw a high island about five miles to the north, its shoulders hunched against the wind. It was Bull Rock, to the north-west of Bantry Bay. I pulled on my stockings and seaboots. The stockings were sodden, the left boot had a two-inch split in it, the chart pencil vanished into the bilge and everywhere stank of ripe cheese.

"What a day," I said to the pigeons.

I let draw the jib and came on course with Sheep Head and the green hills of County Cork on the port bow. The wind went down and veered west, and at eleven the Fastnet light was winking at me through the forestays every five seconds. When its beams were painting the whole mainsail I hove-to again and made a pot of tea. I drank the tea and fed the birds more rice. We were lying near where the Finnish barque *Moshulu* had lain becalmed on a summer's day in 1939 after a passage of ninety days from South Australia at the close of what was to be the last grain race under sail. Here, Eric Newby, the only Englishman in the crew, had found it difficult to converse in his native tongue with

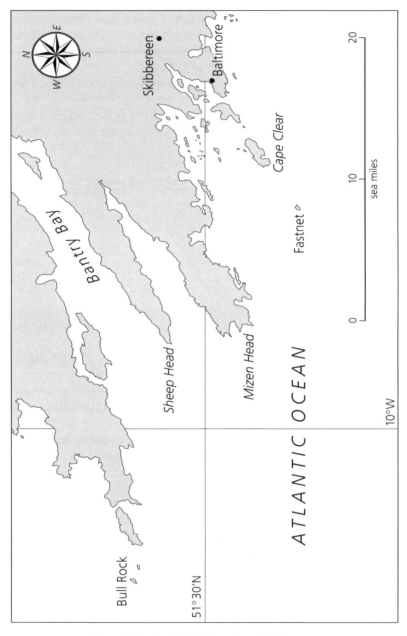

Chart 9: Ireland: Bull Rock to Baltimore.

five men who had rowed nine miles from the village of Crookhaven to speak with them in English about – among other things – the shortage of rain, and had pulled away from *Moshulu* with a bottle of the Captain's rum.

Well, I had sailed to the same part of the Atlantic Ocean from Bermuda in thirty-one days with only two pigeons and a dolphin as fitful – and largely silent – company, and my rum bottle had been emptied long since, and so perhaps it was only to be expected that my voice had become a little rusty.

"Look, we're almost home," I croaked, though Southwold was still all of thirteen hundred miles away.

Thirty-two days after leaving Bermuda *Kylie* nodded past a white pillar called Lot's Wife into Baltimore harbour. I anchored in one and a half fathoms near the town and lit a pipe. My eyes took in the deep rich greens of the hills but I felt no desire to go ashore. I had become so used to looking at sky and sea that during the last few days the very existence of land had seemed open to question, and the passage had drained me of curiosity. Now that I had got close to its green hills, Ireland looked no more substantial than the backdrop of the Never Land in *Peter Pan*. I had the feeling that, if I walked up to the grey cottages and green hills and put out my hands to touch them, I would find they were painted on gauze.

Tristram and Iseult craned above the coaming and clucked heartily, but they too showed no desire to leave. Cooing softly, they preened a few feathers. Before long, all three of us slipped into a doze.

I was woken by tappings on the hull. John Campbell was alongside on a windsurfer.

"Anything the matter?" he said. "I thought you would have been ashore hours ago."

"Yes?"

"So, come along with you – and bring your dirty washing."

"Yes," I said again. Then I cleared my throat and said less hoarsely, "I'll follow after you in a moment."

When he had gone I unlashed the dinghy from the coachroof and gathered up the birds. Their eyes looked into mine with a new brightness. I tried to speak to them for what I knew would be the last time, but for a while the words wouldn't come out.

"It's over," I got out, finally. "What happens next is up to you. From now on, you have to make your own way home."

I threw them upwards. They flew a small circle high above the mast before heading north-westwards, following the road to Skibbereen.

33

Epilogue

Anglesey swam towards me swathed in pink tulle, followed less romantically by the Isle of Man, which struck out through boiling seas girdled in bladderwrack. Tiree and the Pentland Skerries fled past in patchy rain like truants in rags. I drank sparkling wine in Edinburgh on the appointed day and more of the same when a light September wind carried *Kylie* into Southwold, where she was seen to her jetty at the top of the tide by a wide-eyed seal.

Three thousand tides have flowed around the shores of the world since the day on which I got back home to England, and as many winds have blown through other islands, some as helpful in their strengths and slants to the people who live on them as the flooding tide and fair wind which carried *Kylie* safely to her berth. Some winds and tides have been helpful, but not, of course, all of them. Though I had supposed at the Bar Cintra Negra that hurricanes hardly happened in Honduras, in November 1998 the worst Central American hurricane for 200 years swept in from Cabo Gracias à Dios and killed five thousand people. The old clapboard houses of The Settlement on Guanaja were swept away. Nearer buildings have been lost too. Here in England, four winters before the Honduran hurricane, a lesser storm combined with a tidal surge to destroy *Kylie*'s jetty on the Blyth river. Later in the same year a gentler tide and a softer but, to me, sadder wind carried *Kylie* herself down to the sea to begin a seventh Atlantic crossing with a new and younger owner.

It is now six years since I last saw *Kylie* or heard any word from Pip. These days, I put to sea in a bigger boat which has an indefatigable engine and a lavatory which flushes. I value these attachments highly, but I miss my spartan little *Kylie* more than I can say.

For – and I have said this already – what matters most is not where you go but how you get there. Sailing a small boat by yourself with the barest few extras to help you may seem a harder way to get around oceans, but it will always be, to my mind, a more engaging one.

Appendix 1
Kylie

Kylie is a Contessa 26 class sloop, designed by David Sadler. The glassfibre hull and deck were built by Jeremy Rogers at Lymington in 1971, with additional stringers and layers of glassfibre as specified by her first owner, R. Playdon, who fitted her out and equipped her as a long-distance cruiser. Her layout, equipment and scantlings differ from the normal production model in several notable respects: the Proctor E50 mast is fitted with mast-steps, and parallel twin forestays lead from a triangular plate at the masthead to a stainless steel channel-bar at the bows. The blade of the teak rudder, which hangs on 1"-diameter bronze pintles, is strengthened by six stainless steel rods. For most of the time I owned her she was not steered by me but by a very reliable Quarter-master wind-vane steering gear.

The cockpit is reduced in volume by a wooden engine-cover, or bridge deck, at its forward end. Above the bridge deck, $3/4$-inch-thick washboards behind stainless steel flanges protect the companionway from the weather. Instead of the usual six winches on standard Contessas, *Kylie* has only three: two in the cockpit and one on the mast.

During the period covered by this book, *Kylie* carried the following ground-tackle:

- a 35-lb Bruce anchor attached to 10 fathoms of $5/16$th chain and 30 fathoms of 8-plait nylon warp;
- a 25-lb CQR anchor, 9 fathoms $5/16$th chain and 25 fathoms 8-plait nylon warp;
- a 12-lb Danforth anchor on $2^1/2$ fathoms $1/4$-inch chain and 30 fathoms braidline;
- a 10-lb Fisherman anchor on $2^1/2$ fathoms $5/16$th chain;
- a 10-lb folding grapnel anchor on $2^1/2$ fathoms $1/4$-inch chain;
- 50 fathoms of braidline on a reel, and two 12-fathom lengths of three-strand polyester for use with any anchor.

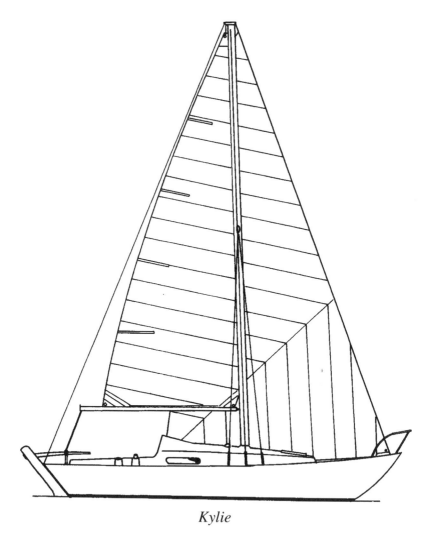

Kylie

Length Overall: 25 ft 8 in
Length on Waterline: 21 ft
Beam: 7 ft 6 in
Draught: 4 ft–4 ft 4 in, depending on weight of stores
Displacement: 5,400–6,000 lbs
Ballast: 2,300 lbs
Sail Area: 304 sq ft

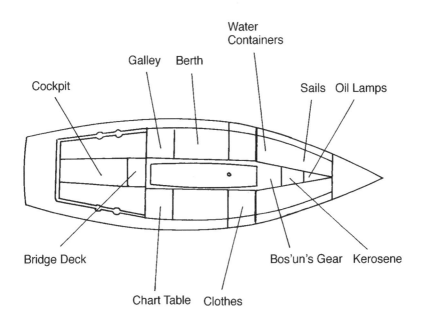

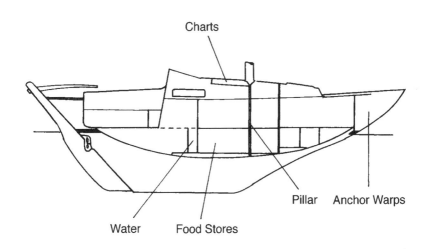

Kylie: interior layout.

The working foresails were carried on deck in two sausage-shaped sailbags attached to the upper guardrail, one on each side forward of the mast. One bag might contain, say, a number one genoa and a storm jib, and in the other would be stowed a number two genoa and a working jib. Apart from the mainsail, which was never removed from the mainboom except when I was, reportedly, in the path of a tornado, the rest of the sails – a ghoster, a spinnaker, a trysail, and a spare genoa and working jib – were carried below decks in what, in other Contessas, was the forecabin.

On standard boats the forecabin contains two berths and a flushing toilet, but during my time in *Kylie* the space was taken up by sailbags, three 5-gallon water-breakers, two 3-gallon kerosene containers and items of bos'un's stores.

My navigation equipment comprised a Bo'sun compass mounted beneath the tiller in the cockpit, a second Plastimo bulkhead compass, a sextant, and a Navstar 2000S satellite navigator. A towed, non-electric Walker log measured the distances run through the water, while the depths were measured by either a Seafarer depthsounder or a leadline.

The small cabin is practical and comfortable. To starboard is a chart-table which accommodates a standard British Admiralty chart folded once, while to port is the galley with its gimballed two-burner Primus stove and its stowage for pans, mugs and plates. The rest of the cabin is taken up by two six-foot berths, beneath which are stowed provisions. Above the foot of each berth is a clothes locker.

Following *Kylie*'s completion in 1971–2, Mr and Mrs Playdon set out for Australia. By the time they had reached the West Indies Mrs Playdon was in an advanced stage of pregnancy, and so they sold *Kylie* and continued their journey homeward by air. John Campbell, her second owner, sailed her back to England, where she was purchased by Simon Hunter with the intention of competing in the 1976 OSTAR, the Observer Transatlantic Race. To get the necessary qualifying experience for OSTAR, Simon succesfully completed the 1975 Azores-and-Back single-handed race.

His experience in the 1976 OSTAR race itself was less happy. He set off for New York by the Southern Route, but weeks of unusually light weather compelled him to abandon the race north of Bermuda and head back eastwards, but not until his 73rd day at sea was he able to make port in the Azores.

After a brief period with a fourth owner, *Kylie* became mine in April 1977, by which time she had already sailed 30,000 miles.

Appendix 2

Glossary of Nautical Terms as Used in This Book

abaft: towards the stern of the vessel in relation to some other part, e.g abaft the beam.

abeam: having a bearing or position at a right angle to the fore-and-aft line of the vessel.

about: A vessel will go about, come about or put about when she goes through the wind from one tack to the other.

a-hull: to lie a-hull is to lie among the waves without sail up and with the tiller lashed to leeward, driven by wind and seas.

a-lee: towards the sheltered side, away from the wind.

astern: in a rearward direction.

autopilot: electrical device which steers automatically to a pre-set compass course.

a-weather: towards the wind.

back, to: (1) to pull the clew of a sail to windward; (2) (of wind) to change anti-clockwise in direction.

beat, to: to sail in a series of zig-zags, with the wind on alternate bows.

Beaufort scale: scale used for measuring the strength of wind, 0 being calm and Force 12 a hurricane (i.e. in excess of 65 knots).

beam: (1) widest transverse dimension of a ship;

(2) transverse member of ship's frame.

bend, to: to fasten one rope to another, or a rope to a spar.

bimini: folding awning above the cockpit.

block: pulley with one or more sheaves.

bobstay: wire or chain running from outer end of bowsprit to stem, to hold down bowsprit against upward pull of forestay.

boom (or mainboom): horizontal spar, extending the foot of mainsail.

bottlescrew: pair of threaded rods turning in a steel tube to tension a stay or a shroud.

bowline: much-used sailors' knot which neither slips nor jams.

bows: foremost part of hull.

bowsprit: spar projecting beyond bows, on which a foresail may be set.

bulkhead: transverse partition of the interior.

bunt: middle part of sail.

cable: (1) strong rope or chain used on anchor; (2) distance of 600 feet, approximately one tenth of nautical mile.

cable locker: stowage place of anchor cable.

cayuco: primitive Central American canoe, made from hollowed-out tree trunk.

cleat: wooden, plastic or metallic deck fitting with arms, on which ropes and lines are fastened.

clew: lower rear corner of fore-and-aft sail.

close hauled: sailing as nearly as possible (about 45 degrees) into the wind.

coachroof: roof of the cabin.

coaming: side of hatch, cabin or cockpit which projects above the deck.

companionway: opening from cabin to cockpit.

course: direction in which a vessel is proceeding, measured in degrees or compass-points from True North, Magnetic North or North as shown on the compass.

cranze iron: steel fitting on the stem at lower end of bobstay.

cringle: metal ring at corners (e.g. luff cringle, clew cringle) of a sail, or along its edges (reef cringles), allowing it to be secured by pins or pendants to the mast, boom or hull.

crutch: support and bearing surface for an oar when rowing.

cutter: single-masted vessel having a mainsail and two foresails.

dead reckoning position or **DR:** arithmetical account of ship's position, using only the course steered and the distance shown on the log, and making no allowance for currents, tidal streams or the wind.

depthsounder: electric instrument for measuring the depth of the water.

dinghy: small open boat, driven by outboard motor, oars or sail.

dividers: measuring-compasses used in chartwork.

dory: flat-bottomed boat, often driven by outboard engine.

draft or **draught:** depth of water which a vessel draws (i.e. becomes afloat); distance from waterline to lowest point of the keel.

draw: to let draw is to adjust the sheets until the sail fills with wind and drives the vessel forward.

fall: hauling part of a rope.

fathom: user-friendly unit of measurement (fingertip-to-fingertip of sideways-stretched arms = 6 feet or 1.8m), now regrettably obsolete, for measuring depths of water or lengths of rope.

fid: conical wooden pin used in splicing.

foresail: any sail forward of the mast.

foretop: mast above foremast.

freeboard: height of ship's side above the water.

gantline: rope taken up the mast to haul up rigging, etc.

genoa: large foresail, the clew of which overlaps the mainsail. *Kylie* carries two genoas, No.1 being the larger.

ghoster: very large, light-weather foresail.

goosewing, to: to run before the wind with a foresail poled-out on each side.

guy: rope used for preventing a pole or boom from swinging.

gybe, to: to cause the mainboom and its sail to swing across the vessel as the stern passes through the wind.

halyard: line which raises or lowers a sail.

hand, to: to take in (sail).

hand-lead: lead weight attached to 20-fathom line, used for discovering the depth of water.

hank: clip for holding the luff of a foresail to a stay.

headboard: triangular metal plate at top corner of mainsail, to which the halyard is attached.

headsail: see **foresail.**

heave-to, to: to set the sails and rudder so that the vessel lies almost stationary.

helm: alternative term for tiller. To up-helm is to move the tiller in the opposite direction to the wind.

hitch: to fasten a rope to a rail or spar with e.g. a clove hitch or a rolling hitch.

Horse Latitudes: area of ocean between the westerly winds and the trade winds, notorious for its calms.

jib: triangular headail set on the forestay.

kedge: secondary, smaller anchor, often used for hauling a grounded vessel off a bank.

ketch: two-masted, fore-and-aft rigged vessel, having the after (or mizzen) mast mounted forward of the sternpost. A double-ended ketch has pointed ends at both bow and stern.

lanyard: short line.

lee shore: shore which lies open to the prevailing wind.

leech: rear edge of a triangular sail.

leeward: in a downwind direction.

leeway: distance a vessel is pushed sideways from her intended course by wind or tide.

log: (1) short for **logbook**; (2) instrument for measuring the distance a vessel has come through the water.

luff: leading edge of a sail.

luff, to: to luff up is to bring the bows to a lesser angle to the wind.

mainsail or **main:** principal sail. A full main is an unreefed mainsail.

make good, to: to cover distance over the seabed.

Mercator's projection: system of drawing sea-maps devised in the sixteenth century by Gerhardus Mercator.

midships, (a)midships: the middle line of the vessel.

mizzen (mast): aftermost mast.

navel pipe: aperture in deck through which anchor cable emerges from below.

painter: line securing dinghy to its parent boat or to the shore.

palm: leather and steel shield which fits across the palm of the hand and bears against the head of the sailmaker's needle.

pendant: line used (for example) in reefing a sail.

point: segment of the compass card, amounting to $11^{1}/_{4}°$. Relative bearings may be in points or degrees, as in, for example, six points from the wind, twenty degrees on the port bow.

point, to, or **to point up:** to sail close(r) to the wind.

port: left-hand side of a vessel as viewed when facing forward.

position-line: terrestial or astronomical bearing on which a vessel is lying.

pulpit: steel safety-frame in the bows, acting as end-support for the guardrails.

reach: point of sailing with the wind abeam.

reef, to: to reduce the area of sail exposed to the wind by tying down one or more of its sections by single-, double-, or deep-reefing it.

rowlock: see **crutch.**

satnav (short for **satellite navigator**): navigation system based on radio transmissions from space satellites.

sextant: hand-held instrument for measuring angles, most commonly those between heavenly bodies and the horizon to obtain a sun-sight or a star-sight.

sheet: line attached to the clew of a sail for trimming it to the wind.

shroud: wire rope running from the hull to the mast, supporting it laterally.

sloop: single-masted vessel with, usually, a single foresail.

sole: floor of cabin or cockpit.

soundings: depths of water shown on the chart. A vessel is in soundings when the navigator is able to measure the depths beneath, or is within the 100-fathom contour marked on the chart.

spinnaker: three-cornered, full-bellied foresail, not attached to the forestay, used when the wind is from abaft the beam.

spreader: strut extending sideways from the mast to broaden the angle between a supporting shroud and its attachment at the masthead.

stanchion: metal post to carry the guardrail or, used below deck, to strengthen the hull.

starboard: right-hand side of a vessel as viewed when facing forward.

stay: wire rope between the hull and masthead, supporting the mast in a fore-and-aft direction.

stern: rear end.

sternsheets: rearmost seats in an open boat.

strake: line of hull planking.

tack: (1) forward lower corner of a sail; (2) closest course to the wind a vessel is able to sail.

tack, to: (1) to bring a vessel's bows through the wind until it is blowing effectively on the other side of the sail; (2) to work upwind in such a manner, going alternately from port tack to starboard tack.

tack tackle: system of blocks and lines to increase the pulling force on the tack of the sail

thimble: plastic or metal eye spliced into a rope to protect it from the wear of another rope or attached shackle.

thole pin: upright bar of wood or metal, acting as leverage to an oar.

tiller: horizontal bar fixed to the rudder-head by which the vessel is steered.

toe rail: part of the hull extending above the deck.

topping lift: line from the masthead supporting the after end of the mainboom.

trade wind: steady, constant winds straddling latitude 20° N and S in the oceans, blowing from the north-east and south-east respectively.

trim, to: to trim sail is to set it to full advantage; to trim ship is to set its bows or stern more deeply or shallowly in the water by re-positioning weight.

veer: in the northern hemisphere, a clockwise change of the wind.

watch: periods of the day aboard ship, most commonly 4 hours in length. The middle (or graveyard) watch is from midnight to 4 a.m.

way: to be under way is to be moving through the water.

weather: used adjectivally to mean a direction into the wind.

weigh, to: to raise the anchor from the bottom.

wheelhouse: central part of the navigation bridge on a merchant ship.

whipping: binding of light line around a rope to stop it untwisting.

winch: mechanism comprising a drum mounted on an axle so as to increase hauling power when tightening sheets and halyards.

windlass: foredeck winch with a drum to accommodate the anchor cable.

yaw, to: to wander from the desired course through the action of wind and sea.

yoke lines: lanyards and shock-cord to dampen stresses on the tiller.